W9-CTO-681

CRITICALLY ACCLAIMED!

Hear is the book that thowzands of those of Polish extrakshun (and prowd of it!) have been waiting for! I red every joke and almost split my sides laffing. I hope that all those other ethnik groops will buy it too. Then they will no that Poles aint as dumb as they think. Their even publishhing books about us. The Italian side ain't so grate tho. Those people could sure use some smarts. But one of the jokes called to mind my garbaageman. It was wunnerful!

—Stanislas Poznanski; Literary Editor
   The Hamtramck Polish-American Bugle

THE OFFICIAL POLISH-ITALIAN JOKEBOOK

compiled and edited by
Larry Wilde

illustrations by
Ron Wing

PINNACLE BOOKS • NEW YORK CITY

THE OFFICIAL POLISH-ITALIAN JOKEBOOK

Text copyright © 1973 by Larry Wilde
Illustrations copyright © 1973 by Pinnacle Books, Inc.

An original Pinnacle Books edition, published for the
first time anywhere.

ISBN: 0-523-00242-4

First printing, September 1973
Second printing, October 1973
Third printing, November 1973
Fourth printing, January 1974

Printed in the United States of America

PINNACLE BOOKS, INC.
275 Madison Avenue
New York, N.Y. 10016

With special thanks to Professor Dan Desmond for his invaluable assistance.

PREFACE

Ethnic jokes have been around since Biblical times. Humor historians claim that man has always poked fun at some race or religious group. It just happens that today these barbed jests are directed toward Americans of Polish and Italian descent.

Through the years, in the United States, other victims have been Jews, Negroes, Germans, Mexicans, Puerto Ricans and the Irish. Not to overlook the Swedes around Minneapolis, Finns near Fitchburg, Massachusetts, and the original Americans, the foot, pony, and cliff Indians.

In the 1880s, newly arrived Sons of Erin were referred to as "micks" and "greenhorns" and were lampooned for their speech, manners, and alleged ignorance.

The following gag is typical of what convulsed the boys down at the corner saloon:

Two Irish ladies were coming back from church. "Me son, Jimmy's comin' home tomorra!" said Mrs. Murphy.

"That's nice!" Replied Mrs. O'Connor. "But I though he was sent up fer five years!"

"That's true!" answered her companion. "But he got time off fer good behavior!"

"Oh, my," said her friend. "It must be a blessin' to you, to know you've got such a fine son!"

During the influx of Spanish speaking people from San Juan, the popular putdown around New York had as its tag a line from a well-known song.

What is the Puerto Rican National Anthem?

(*Singing*) We'll take Manhattan, the Bronx and Staten Island, too! . . .

Probably the longest continuous tirade of mockery (*a couple of thousand years*) has been aimed at those of the Jewish faith. Witness this once typical example of anti-Semitic derision:

How did the Grand Canyon come about?

A Jew dropped a penny down a Gopher hole.

If that below-the-belt jab wasn't painful enough, here's a little solar plexus punch from out of the dark, prejudiced past:

Why do Jews have large noses?

Because the air is free.

Jokes have become so sophisticated over the years it is now possible to offend several groups at one time. A good case in point is this story being told around Southern California:

Why is Sunday morning the best time to be on the Los Angeles Freeways?

The Catholics are in church.

The Protestants are still asleep.

The Jews are in Palm Springs.

The Indians are restricted to the reservation.

The Chinese are stuffing fortune cookies.

The Blacks are in jail.

And the Mexicans can't get their cars started.

Dating back to the days of vaudeville, Polish-Americans around Buffalo, Detroit and Milwaukee suffered humiliating cracks about themselves. (Little knowing that one day Polish jokes would become a national craze.)

The wisecrack is a traditional form of the American jest. The core of its effectiveness comes from somebody being the butt of the joke, for it is always easier to laugh when someone else is being ridiculed.

And yet isn't that the greatness of America? That we live in a land where telling any kind of joke is permitted? That our right to free speech enables us to poke fun at even the most sacred elements of our social and cultural value system?

Psychiatrists contend that the higher the intelligence the greater the sense of humor. And therein lies the key. The ability to laugh at oneself.

Of course, when one is a member of a minority and the object of the barb, one must have a super king-sized funny bone. Remember, it's all in fun.

Let's take our example from the broad-minded mother who advised her eldest daughter, in case she ever got raped: "If you can't do anything about it, you might as well lie back and enjoy it!"

On the following pages you will find the best—or the worst, depending on your sensibilities and sense of humor—of the Polish and Italian jokes currently making the rounds throughout the United States.

Please! Lie back and enjoy it!

Larry Wilde
September, 1973

ABOUT THE AUTHOR

Larry Wilde, popular nightclub and television comedian, has performed at most of the major entertainment spots in the United States, Canada and Australia. He has appeared with Debbie Reynolds, Vikki Carr, Wayne Newton, Sonny & Cher, Ann-Margret and Pat Boone. The record shops have featured his comedy album, "The Joker Is Wilde," for Dot Records and he makes regular appearances on TV with Johnny Carson, Merv Griffin, and Mike Douglas.

Born in Jersey City, New Jersey, Larry earned his bachelor's degree at the University of Miami, Florida. His writing credits include articles for magazines and professional journals, as well as authoring *The Great Comedians Talk About Comedy*, a best-selling book on comedic technique.

Mr. Wilde resides in Hollywood, where, between Las Vegas engagements, concert appearances and university lectures, he conducts a comedy workshop.

THE OFFICIAL
POLISH
JOKEBOOK

PIROGI

What's green, purple, orange, chartreuse, pink, and red?

A Polish housewife going to church on Sunday.

*   *   *

How many Polacks does it take to paint a house?

1,001.
One to hold the brush and 1,000 to move the house up and down.

*   *   *

What happened to the Polish National Library?

Somebody stole the book.

*   *   *

Polack Being Interviewed for a Job:

Interviewer: Your name is Bob?
Polack: Yes.
Interviewer: Do you spell it with two o's?

*   *   *

Why don't they have any ice cubes in Poland?

The inventor died and took the recipe with him.

*   *   *

What is the smallest building in Poland?

The Polish Hall of Fame.

*   *   *

Brudzewa and Wlassak bought a Country Squire station wagon with wooden sides. When they got it home, they ripped off all the wood paneling. When they'd finished, Brudzewa said, "You know, I like wagon better when it was in box!"

*   *   *

How do Polish dogs get snubbed noses?
From chasing parked cars.

       *   *   *

What do the numbers 1776 and 1492 have in common?

They are adjoining rooms at the Warsaw Hilton.

       *   *   *

Barry Glazer, Exec Producer and Director of Dick Clark's "American Bandstand" TV show, swears this happened at a taping:

"Harry, I got a great new Polish joke for you," said a cameraman to the floor manager.

"Okay, but just be careful," warned Harry. "Remember, I'm Polish!"

"All right," replied the cameraman, "I'll tell it to you very slowly."

       *   *   *

Polish Ponderosa: Kosciuosko Park.

       *   *   *

Comedian-Dialectician Jeremy Vernon repeated this classic to me backstage at the Century Plaza Hotel: Kowalski and Resnicki were digging a cesspool. "How come we down here and Irish guy is upstairs in clear air?" said Kowalski. "All he got do is pull up bucket."

"By Joe, you right!" agreed Resnicki. "I go up and find out!"

"It'd be easier for me," said the Irishman, "to illustrate than to explain the reason." *He placed his hand flat against the wall and said:* "Hit my hand as hard as you can." Resnicki did. At the last second the Irishman yanked his hand away and Resnicki smashed his fist into the brick wall.

Down in the cesspool again, he said, "Kowalski, you want know why Irish guy is up there and we down here?"

"Yes!" said Kowalski.

"It be easier for me to illustrate than to explain reason." *Resnicki held his hand in front of his face and said:* "Hit my hand with shovel, hard as you can!"

* * *

Comic Lou Alexander tells about Kuchinski walking into the doctor's office with a frog on his head. "What seems to be the problem?" asked the physician.

And the frog said, "Well, it's about this wart on my behind."

*   *   *

Why does it take five men to give a Polack a shower?

One to hold him and four to spit.

*   *   *

Janicki and Bolewicz were strolling along the beach. Suddenly a sea gull flying overhead dropped a load. It hit Janicki right in the eye.

"I'll go get some toilet paper," offered Bolewicz.

"Don't bother," said Janicki. "He's probably miles away by now!"

*   *   *

Morris Diamond, Beverly Hills Records prez and cocktail party raconteur, tells about the man sitting next to a Polish woman on an airplane. She was carrying a baby in her arms. The man said to her,

"Lady, that is the ugliest baby I've ever seen! It looks like a monkey!"

The incensed woman called over the stewardess and said, "This man just insulted me! He called my baby a monkey!"

"Don't be upset," soothed the hostess. "I'll get you a drink and then I'll bring your lunch . . . and here's a banana for your baby!"

*　　*　　*

What do the call a dance attended by a bunch of Polacks?

A goof ball.

*　　*　　*

Why wasn't Christ born in Poland?

They couldn't find three wise men and a virgin.

*　　*　　*

Ned Sukin, New Jersey's top liquor salesman, tells buyers about the Chicagoan who goes to the doctor for a brain transplant. "If you'd like to have a Jewish brain, it'll cost $10,000!" explained the

M.D. "If you want a Polish brain, you'll have to pay $100,000!"

"I can understand the Jewish brain costing ten grand," said the Windy City resident, "Those people are pretty smart. But why is the other one so expensive?"

"Ah, Hah!" said the physician, "The Polish brain has never been used!"

*   *   *

What do they call a hoola hoop?

A teething ring for big-mouthed Polacks.

*   *   *

What is a Polish queer?

A guy who would rather go out with girls than go pick mushrooms.

*   *   *

Actress-interior decorator Cara Williams saves this one for special new friends: Poles up in arms over the slanderous remarks about their intelligence, finally forced NASA to employ a Polish astronaut. On his first mission he was sent into space with just a monkey and told to watch the red light on his panel. When it lit up, he was to follow the prerecorded instructions. The green light provided commands for the monkey.

An hour after liftoff, the green light flashed and instructed the monkey: "You are now at stage one. Record speed. Regulate radiograph. Release retroactive regenerators!" And he did.

In a little while the green light lit up again and the monkey followed his orders: "Fire rockets. Adjust oxygen supply. Take temperature, blood pressure, and check pulse rate."

Four hours later, the red light came on and the Polish astronaut breathlessly awaited his first command. Over the loudspeaker came these instructions: "Feed the monkey!"

*　　*　　*

Polish National Bank:　Pole Vault.

*　　*　　*

How do you make Polish Shishkabob?

You shoot a flaming arrow into a garbage can.

*　　*　　*

FOR SALE

ONLY $25.00

LEFT HANDED POLISH TARGET PISTOL ONLY USED ONCE

Why does a Polack keep his fly open?

In case he has to count to eleven.

* * *

O'Donald: You Polacks are all stupid.
Zabriski: That not true. We just like
everybody else.
O'Donald: Okay, then. What's your name?
Zabriski: (*Begins counting on fingers
and then says*) "Stanley."
O'Donald: Stanley is not sixteen letters.
Zabriski: No . . . (*counting on fingers
again*) "Happy birthday to
you, Happy birthday to you
. . ."

* * *

Mann Scharf, popular Hollywood pub-
licist, makes this contribution: Grabowski
and Molinski were walking down Eighth
Avenue and met a priest who had his arm
in a cast.

"How it happen?" asked Grabowski.

"I slipped in the bathtub and broke it,"
replied the father.

The two men continued their stroll and Grabowski said, "Hey, what is bathtub?"

"How I know," answered Molinski, "I not Catholic!"

*   *   *

Polish Martini: A marble in a glass of 7-Up.

*   *   *

How does one Polack find another Polack in the dark?

Wonderful.

*   *   *

How did the first 1,000 Polacks cross the ocean?

One swam across and the other 999 walked across on the dead fish.

*   *   *

Why can't Polacks eat dill pickles?

They can't get their heads in the jar.

*   *   *

How did the Polack get all those holes in his forehead?

Learning to eat with a fork.

*   *   *

Garbinski and Zywacki were sitting in a saloon, talking politics. "What would you do with Red China?" asked Garbinski.

"I'd put it on a purple tablecloth," replied Zywacki.

*   *   *

Jay Burton, scribe for Milton Berle, Carol Burnett and a host of other TV comics, swears this is the only Polish joke he ever wrote:

What is the capitol of Poland?

Forty Cents.

*   *   *

The four most dangerous people in the world:

A Jew with an attorney.
A Greek with sneakers.
A Frenchman with a jagged tooth.
A Polack with a credit card.

*   *   *

Zabiski:	Hey, Custak, if you can tell me how many chickens I have in this bag, I give you both of them!
Custak:	Three!
Zabiski:	No fair! You looked in the bag!

*　　*　　*

A steel mill had a football game between the Poles and the Italians. They played all afternoon with neither team able to score. Suddenly, it was five o'clock, the factory whistle blew and the Italian team walked off the field. Three plays later, the Polacks scored a touchdown.

*　　*　　*

What do they call a swimming pool full of Polish girls?

Bay of Pigs.

*　　*　　*

Everyone knows that Cortez discovered Mexico and Columbus discovered America, but who discovered Poland?

The Roto Rooter man.

*　　*　　*

Polish Flag: Mop.

*   *   *

Lewis Wildman, Jersey City's greeting card king, tells about Pilzudski being a contestant on a television quiz show. "For $1,000," said the M.C., "tell us the meaning of Easter!"

Pilzudski paused for a moment and then said: "This man come out of ground . . ."

"That's it!" shouted the master of ceremonies. "You've won the thousand dollars!"

". . . And turns around," continued the Polack, "and if he see his shadow . . ."

*   *   *

Polish-Americans, offended by the viciousness of the jokes told about them, are quick to remind friends of the bravery of the Polish people during World War II.

The Poles are reputed to have barehandedly thrown sticks of dynamite into the hordes of attacking German soldiers. The Nazis then caught the sticks of dynamite, lit them, and threw them back.

*   *   *

Investment Counselor Gary Judas tells about the Polish army sergeant who called his platoon to attention and shouted: "Men, after three week it be time to change underwear! Kozlow, you change with Banacek. Banacek you change with Linkowski. Linkowski you change with. . . ."

* * *

What do they call a Polack chasing a garbage truck?

A Galloping Gourmet.

* * *

Why did the Polack throw the clock out the window?

He wanted to see time fly.

* * *

Totie Fields got a scream with this on stage at the Riviera Hotel in Las Vegas:
Why does a Polack eat beans for dinner on Saturday night?

So he can take a bubble bath Sunday morning.

* * *

Rancho Park golf pro, Ed Coleman, tells about the American, Frenchman and Pole in France who were sentenced to death on the guillotine. The judge said to the American, "Do you have any last words?" "Drop dead!" snapped the Yank. The judge signaled for the sentence to be carried out. The executioner pulled the lever and as the crowd gaped in astonishment, the giant blade came to a screeching halt three inches from severing the victim's head. "It is God's will," cried the astounded judge. "Let the American go free!"

They put the Frenchman on the block and the judge asked, "What are your final remarks?" "Go to hell!" the Frenchman shouted. Again the signal. The razor-sharp blade dropped and again it miraculously stopped only a quarter inch from the condemned prisoner's head. "It is the will of God," exclaimed the judge. "Set him free!"

Now they placed the Pole in position. "Before you are beheaded," said the judge, "do you have any last words?" "Yeah," said the Polack. "If you put a little grease in those grooves, blade comes down much easier!"

*   *   *

"... put a little grease in those grooves, blade comes down much easier!"

What does it say on the bottom of a Coke bottle in Poland?

Open other end.

*   *   *

Why does it take five Polacks to screw in a light bulb?

One to hold the light and four to turn the ladder.

*   *   *

Why is Santa Claus Polish?

Who else would wear a red suit?

*   *   *

How do you tell the property values in Poland?

The farther from Warsaw the more expensive.

*   *   *

Why does it take ten Polacks to hang a picture?

One to hold the nail and nine to push the wall.

*   *   *

Cyrankiewicz was having his eyes examined.

"Read the bottom line," said the optometrist.

"Hey," said the Polack, "I know that fellow!"

*　　*　　*

Polish woman was told by the doctor to come back the next day with a sample of her urine. She returned with a bedpan filled to the top.

"Mrs. Witkowski," admonished the physician, "How could you walk through the streets, carrying a bedpan full of urine!"

"What you mean *walk*," she replied, "I took bus!"

*　　*　　*

Los Angeles appliance tycoon Monte Mellman regales customers with the one about Zawadski the lumberjack who wanted to buy a saw. The clerk said, "This is our best model. It'll cut down fifty trees in six hours."

Zawadski bought it, but returned to the store next evening, his face flushed with anger. "You cheat me," he complained.

"You say this saw cut down fifty trees in six hour. I only cut thirty-five and it take me all day!"

The bewildered clerk took the cord attached to the saw and plugged it into an electric socket. He then pushed a button which started the motor. The Polack jumped back and shouted, "What be that noise?"

* * *

Polish homosexual walking down the street, carrying a midget under his arm. He meets another member of dubious sexuality and says, "Say, Arnold, want a drag before I throw him away?"

* * *

Mojalewski met his friend Sawicki on Third Avenue, laughing his head off. "Why you laugh?" asked Mojalewski.

"I think about dumbbell I see this morning," replied Sawicki.

"What you mean?" quizzed Mojalewski.

"This morning alarm clock forget to ring. Wife and I oversleep. It be after nine o'clock when I wake up. I jump into clothes without waking wife and just be ready to leave when bedroom door open. In come Iceman!"

"What you do?"

"I almost die laughing!"

"Why?" asked Mojalewski.

"It be so damn funny!" answered the Polack. "Can you imagine guy be so dumb, he comes into bedroom looking for icebox!"

*   *   *

How many Polacks does it take to make popcorn?

Twenty.
One to hold the pan and nineteen to shake the stove.

*   *   *

Savings and loan manager John Ekblad tells about the Cherokee chief who comes to California looking for a place to live. An unscrupulous real estate broker sells the Indian an outhouse.

Three days later, the agent drives by and sees a television antenna on the roof. A week later, he sees a second one.

"I notice you've got another TV antenna up on your roof," said the real estate man. "How come?"

"I rented out the basement to a Polack," replied the chief.

*   *   *

Potowski and Zablocki were working their first day in a coal mine. Potowski turned on his headlamp and said, "I bet you $5 you can't climb all the way up that beam of light."

"Oh, yes, I could," answered Zablocki.

"For $5 I say you can't."

"Five dollars I say I can!"

"Okay, go ahead and climb it."

"You can't fool me," said Zablocki. "I get halfway up and you'd turn the damn thing off!"

*　　*　　*

Billy Barty, prince of the little people, tells about the two Polish astronauts who were circling the Earth in outer space. One of them was sent outside the capsule to walk around. An hour later he wanted to re-enter, so he knocked on the door. The Polack inside said, "Who's there?"

*　　*　　*

Russia decided they wanted to have their own Disneyland. So they built a fence around Poland.

*　　*　　*

Polish Combat Soldier

Polish underarm deodorant—Raid.

*   *   *

A young Polish girl was taking the state board examination to become a nurse. The doctor asked her, "How do you wash genitals?"

"The same way you wash Jews!" she replied innocently.

*   *   *

Phillip Moyer of El Modena, California tells about the lady who was showing a contractor through the second floor of her new house to advise him what colors to paint the rooms. "I'd like the bathroom done in white!"

The contractor walked over to the window and shouted: "Green up! Green up!"

"I want the bedroom in blue!" continued the woman.

The contractor yelled out the window, "Green up! Green up!"

"The halls should be done in beige!" Again the man barked out the window, "Green up! Green up!"

"Will you stop that!" ordered the woman angrily. "Every time I give you a color I want, you shout 'Green up!' What in God's name does that mean?"

"I'm terribly sorry, ma'am!" explained the contractor. "But I've got three Polacks down below putting in the lawn!"

* * *

"What will you charge me to paint my house," asked the man of a Polish painter.

"Twelve dollar a day!" replied Bratkowski.

"Good Lord!" exclaimed the home owner. "I wouldn't pay Michelangelo that price!"

"I tell you one thing, by Joe," said the Polack, "if that Wop is doing job for less, he no be member of union!"

* * *

Polish Cocktail: A mushroom in a glass of beer.

* * *

Shelley Graves, Grand Rapids, Michigan, tells about the three Polacks who were standing one on top of the other, trying to measure a flagpole.

A man passing by yelled up to them,

"Why don't you take the pole, lay it down on the ground and measure it."

"We not want measure *length*," said the Polack in charge. "We want measure *height!*"

*   *   *

Theatrical rep, Ken Grayson, says it is a historical fact that Diogenes went all around the world carrying a lamp, trying to find an honest man. When he got to Poland, they stole his lamp.

*   *   *

What's Polish surf and turf?

Herring and Kalbasi.

*   *   *

Linkowski and Kawecki were driving from Detroit to Cleveland. Just outside the city limits they saw a sign: "Clean Rest Rooms." By the time they got to Cleveland they cleaned 147 rest rooms.

*   *   *

Financial adviser Steve Gerber asks: What happens when you cross a Jew with a Polack?

You get a janitor who owns the building.

*   *   *

Giovani tells Polski that he passed the citizenship test by writing all the answers on the waistband of his undershorts.

Polski borrows Giovani's underwear and shows up the next day for the exam. He was the only one in the office, so the clerk decided to give him the test orally.

"How many original colonies were there in America?"

Polski, pretending he was thinking, faced about, turned over the waistband of his shorts and then answered, "34!"

The bewildered examiner figured the poor man was nervous and went on: "What are the colors of the flag?"

Again Polski checked his shorts and replied, "Brown and white!"

The public official decided to try one last question. "Who was the first president of the United States?"

The Polack glanced quickly at his undershorts and then proudly proclaimed:

"J. C. Penney!"

*   *   *

Did you hear about the . . .

—Two Polacks who hijacked a submarine and asked for a million dollars and two parachutes?

*   *   *

—Polack who went to a masquerade ball and at midnight when the hostess asked him to take off his mask, he said, "I ain't got one on!"

*   *   *

Did you hear about the . . .

—Polack who shot an arrow in the air?

Missed.

*   *   *

—Polish woman who had a hysterectomy so she'd stop having grandchildren?

*   *   *

—Polack who was two hours late because the escalator got stuck?

*   *   *

—Nervous Polish surgeon who was finally discharged from the hospital?

It wasn't so much all the patients he lost ... it was those deep gashes he made in the operating table.

*   *   *

Did you hear about the ...

—Polish woman who made her toilet into an end table?

She moved the sofa into the bathroom.

*   *   *

—Polack who stayed up all night studying for his urine test?

*   *   *

43

—Fleet-footed Polish girl?

She only ran after sailors.

*   *   *

—Polish nurse who drove right through a red light. A cop stopped her and said, "Don't you know what a red light stands for?" "Of course," said the nurse. "A bedpan! What else?"

*   *   *

Did you hear about the . . .

—Polack whose wife had triplets and he went out looking for the other two guys?

*   *   *

—Polish athlete at the Olympics who won a gold medal and went out and had it bronzed?

*   *   *

—Polack who invented the wheelbarrow so he could learn to walk on his hind legs?

*   *   *

—Polish farmer's daughter who suffered a fate worse than death to pay off the villain who held a mortgage on the family farm—and enjoyed it so much she went out looking for the guy who held the second mortgage?

*   *   *

Did you hear about the . . .

—Polack in the hotel who complained about the noise next door?
"I'm sorry, sir," said the desk clerk. "They're holding an Elks convention."
"I don't care if they've got him by the antlers," barked the Polack, "I wanna get some sleep!"

*   *   *

—Polish Kamikazi pilot who returned safely from forty missions?

*   *   *

—Polish prostitute who didn't vote?

She didn't care who got in.

*   *   *

—Polish glass blower who inhaled?

Now he's got a pane in the stomach.

*   *   *

Did you hear about the . . .

—Negro boys running toward their swimming hole, shouting, "The last one in is a dirty Polack!?"

*   *   *

—Polish race driver at Indianapolis who had to make seventy-five pit stops?

Three for fuel.
Four to change tires.
And sixty-eight to ask directions.

* * *

—Polack who wouldn't go out with his wife
because he found out she was married?

* * *

Did you hear about the . . .

—Polack who was asked if he'd like to
become a Jehovah's Witness?

He said he couldn't because he didn't see
the accident.

* * *

—Polish girl who thought a sanitary belt
was a drink from a clean shot glass?

* * *

—Polack who smelled good only on one side?

He didn't know where to buy any Left Guard.

*　　*　　*

—Polack who ordered a pizza?

He was asked if he wanted it cut into four or eight pieces. He said, "Make it four. I'll never be able to eat eight pieces."

*　　*　　*

Did you hear about the . . .

—Polish woman who shopped for three days looking for wheels for her miscarriage?

*　　*　　*

—Polack who thought Vat 69 was the pope's phone number?

*　　*　　*

—Polish housewife who got mad at her husband because he was off shooting craps and she didn't know how to cook them?

* * *

—Polish woman who wanted to turn in her menstrual cycle for a Honda?

* * *

Did you hear about the . . .

—Polish plumber who looked at Niagara Falls and said, "Give me time and I could fix it!"

* * *

—Polish efficiency expert who has all the boys at the plant on their toes lately?

He raised the urinals twelve inches.

* * *

—Polack who saw a movie and then waited four hours by the side door for the star to come out?

* * *

—Polack who went up to a street-sprinkling truck and told the driver his car was leaking?

* * *

Did you hear about the . . .

—Polack who asked to be buried at sea?

His son drowned trying to dig his grave.

* * *

—Polack who thought Peter Pan was something you put under your bed at night?

* * *

—Polish girl who lost her mind?

For ten years she worked in a house of ill repute. Then she found out the rest of the girls got paid.

*　　*　　*

—Polack who took his pregnant wife to a supermarket because he heard that they had free delivery?

*　　*　　*

Did you hear about the . . .

—Polack who came home after being a prisoner of war for five years?

When he got off the plane a beautiful blonde walked up to him and said, "How'd you like to have something you haven't had in years?" And he said, "Don't tell me you've got a filter cigarette?"

*　　*　　*

—Polack who was so lazy he married a pregnant woman?

*   *   *

—Polack who hijacked an Israeli plane and demanded one million dollars in pledges?

*   *   *

Did you hear about the...

—Polish girl who was so ugly that when she walked into a room the mice jumped up on chairs?

*   *   *

—Polack who went down to city hall for his driver's license?

It was so crowded he got on the wrong line.
Now he's the only guy in the world married to a Toyota.

*   *   *

Polish Brassiere

—Polish kidnapper who sent his hostage out to collect the ransom?

* * *

—Polish pickpocket who only has one finger?

He steals nothing but key rings.

* * *

—Polack who was so bowlegged he could walk down a bowling alley while the game was going on?

* * *

Did you hear about the . . .

—Polack who opened up a travel agency and went broke in two weeks?

He kept trying to book reservations on the *Titanic, Lusitania* and the *Andrea Dorea.*

* * *

—Polish girl whose bags under her eyes were so big, her nose looked like it was wearing a saddle?

* * *

Did you hear about the ...

—Polack who stepped in a pile of cow dung and started crying?

He thought he was melting.

* * *

—High class Polish girl who only had her number written in telephone booths on the east side of town?

* * *

—Polish airliner that crashed?

It ran out of coal.

* * *

Did you hear about the . . .

—Polish girl who took a job as a model in Alaska?

She poses for totem poles.

*   *   *

—Polish street cleaner who went berserk following a merry-go-round?

*   *   *

—Polish girl who was so bowlegged she looked like one bite out of a doughnut?

*   *   *

—Polack who kept laughing when they put him in the electric chair?

He said, "The joke's on you. You've got the wrong guy!"

*   *   *

—Polish girl who couldn't understand why she was blessed with twins, since she had never been on a double date?

*   *   *

—Polack who told his wife to get something on the TV set?

So she went out and hocked it.

*   *   *

—Three-fingered Polish pickpocket?

He only steals bowling balls.

*   *   *

—Polish surgeon who worked in a doughnut factory?

He made the incision then someone else put the jelly in.

*   *   *

Did you hear about the...

—Polish cop who gave out twenty-two parking tickets before he found out he was in a drive-in movie?

*   *   *

—Polack who hates dogs?

He went to a masquerade ball as a lamp post.

*   *   *

—Polish plumber's daughter?

Every time someone told her a spicy joke her cheeks flushed.

*   *   *

Did you hear about the...

—Polish coal miner who takes a bath just once a week?

Then he bottles the bath water and sells it for ink.

*   *   *

—Polish girl everybody thought was such a happy kid because she was always smiling?

Then they found out her false teeth were too big.

*   *   *

—Polack who couldn't count to ten?
One of his fingers was missing.

*   *   *

—Polish girl who never wore a necklace?
She just braided her wrinkles.

GAWOOMPKI

How many Polacks does it take to make love?

Three.
Two to do it and one to read the instructions out of the book.

*   *   *

Why did the Polack stop at the house of ill repute?

He was waiting for the light to change.

*   *   *

What happened when they dropped the Atom Bomb on Warsaw?

It did $10.15 worth of damage.

*   *   *

Polish Sex Manual

How does a Polish mother put on her child's underwear?

Yellow in front, brown in back.

*   *   *

Why are Polish mothers so strong and square-shouldered?

From raising dumbbells.

*   *   *

What's harder than getting six pregnant Polish women in a Volkswagen?

Getting six Polish women pregnant in a Volkswagen.

*   *   *

Two Secretaries at Lunch:

Gloria: I was raped last night by a Polack.
Helen: How do you know he was Polish?
Gloria: I had to help him.

*   *   *

Two Poles Walking Abreast

The Morning After:

Italian Girl: My mother would die if she found out.

Spanish Girl: Now I will love you always.

Russian Girl: My body belongs to you; my soul will always belong to the state!

German Girl: After we go to beer garden, yah?

Swedish Girl: Aye tank aye go home now.

French Girl: For this I get a new dress, oui?

Chinese Girl: Now you know it's not true.

English Girl: Rather pleasant, what?

American Girl: Damn, I must've been really crocked. What'd you say your name was?

Jewish Girl: I'll have to go to the beauty parlor today!

Polish Girl: Can you really get me a screen test?

*   *   *

A Madison Avenue advertising agency conducted a survey in Europe to find out which was the most popular feminine hygiene spray. They discovered that in France it was a product called "Feminique." In

England, it was "Pristine." And in Poland, it was "Janitor in a Drum."

*   *   *

Polish couple had a double ring ceremony. They were married in a bathtub.

*   *   *

Polish Wedding Good Luck Guide for the Bride:

Something old,
Something new,
Something borrowed,
Something blue.
Something red,
Something orange,
Something purple,
Something...

*   *   *

How Can You Tell the Groom at a Polish Wedding?

—He's the one with the dirty T-shirt.

*   *   *

—He's the one with the white bowling shoes.

* * *

—He's the one not wearing a bowling shirt.

* * *

—He's the one wearing a tuxedo and combat boots.

* * *

How can you tell the bride at a Polish wedding?

She's the one with the braided armpits and sequins on her sneakers.

* * *

When Sophie returned from her honeymoon, she telephoned the doctor. "Those birth control pills you gave me aren't working!"

"What do you mean, not working?" asked the surprised physician. "I just gave them to you a week ago!"

"Well," replied the newlywed. "They keep falling out!"

* * *

How can you tell the mother-in-law at a Polish wedding?

She's the one on her hands and knees picking up the rice.

*   *   *

After making violent love to his wife for over an hour, Wladislaw said to her, "Why the hell did I ever marry you? You've got nothing on top . . . nothing on bottom . . ."

"Look," she gasped. "Get off my back!"

*   *   *

Ernie Medwig of Pittsburgh tells about Prapowski coming home and finding his wife in bed with another man. The Pole took out a gun from the drawer and put it to his head. The wife's lover jumped up and shouted, "Hey, what're you doing?"

"Shut up!" said the Polack. "You're next!"

*   *   *

What brings tears to a Polish mother's eyes?

When she buys her son his first athletic supporter.

*   *   *

71

Jack Stokes, Southern California golf pro, always gets a big laugh with this one: Zimbriski and Raczkiewicz were hunting game out in the woods. Suddenly they came across a stark-naked blonde sitting on a tree stump.

"Hey," shouted Zimbriski. "Are you game?"

"Yes!" replied the woman.

So he shot her.

* * *

Rafael Vega, of Casa Vega, the great Sherman Oaks Mexican eatery, provided this gem: An obstetrician called on Mrs. Sobieski two days after she had delivered a husky youngster and found her holding an ice bag to her bosom.

"Trouble with your breasts?" asked the M.D.

"No trouble, doctor," replied the woman. "I do this to keep milk fresh!"

* * *

"Hows your wife?" asked Cusick.

"She's up in bed with laryngitis," replied Novack.

"Oh," retorted his friend. "Is that Greek bastard around again!

* * *

Polish Peeping Tom

Bridegroom to the hotel clerk, "How much do we owe for the room?"

"Five bucks apiece!"

Smolinski handed him fifty dollars.

*   *   *

Talent manager Arnold Mills tells about the love-sick Romeo who went to a doctor and said, "I'm dating a Polish girl and so I want to become a Pole!"

"That's a little unusual," said the dumbfounded physician. "But if that's what you want, okay. In order to become a real Polack I'll have to remove half your brain!"

"I'll do it!" agreed the young lover.

After the operation, the doctor revived his patient and said, "I'm terribly sorry! By mistake, I removed three-quarters of your brain!"

"Oh, mama, mia!" shouted the bewildered boy.

*   *   *

Have you heard about the sixty-second Polish sex maniac?

Got a minute?

*   *   *

74

Cad: A Polack who doesn't tell his wife he's sterile until after she's pregnant.

* * *

Chicago exec sec Sandy Bylczynski tells about the Polish couple who planned to get married and went to the doctor for their blood test. The M.D. then tried to explain sex to them. The boy just listened with a dumb expression on his face.

So the doctor took his fianceé over to the examination table, had her lie down and then made love to her. "Now do you understand?" asked the physician.

"Yeah," said the Polack. "But how often do I have to bring her in?"

* * *

Miss Konarski walked into a bank, carrying a large paper bag filled with nickels, dimes and quarters. "Did you hoard all this money by yourself?" inquired the teller.

"No," said the girl. "My sister whored half of it!"

* * *

Skiing: A Polish Love-In.

*   *   *

Private Polachek, of the Foreign Legion, hadn't seen a woman in years. "I'm getting pretty frustrated," said the Legionnaire to his sergeant. "What am I going to do?"

"See that camel over there," answered the NCO. "The men are supposed to use that animal when they need to relieve themselves!"

That night the sergeant was awakened by the camel squealing and screeching. He discovered Polachek kissing and hugging the animal and having a great time.

"What're you doing?" shouted the sergeant. "You're supposed to take the camel and ride it into town where all the women are!"

*   *   *

What do they call a stork that delivers Polish babies?

A dope peddler.

*   *   *

Polish marriage proposal: "You're gonna have a *what?*"

*   *   *

While selling construction equipment, Bob Bernard tells this one: Mayor Lindsay declared war on the rats in New York. His Honor ordered the health inspector to send nine Polish exterminators down into the sewers to wipe out the rodents.

A month later, only six of the nine Poles came back. "What happened to the other three men?" demanded the mayor.

"They defected to the enemy!" exclaimed the inspector. "And out of the six that returned, two brought back war brides!"

*   *   *

How can you tell which kid in the first grade class is Polish?

The one with the rusty zipper and the yellow sneakers.

*   *   *

Why did the Polish kids stop playing in the sandbox?

The cats kept trying to bury them.

* * *

Real estate broker Carol Malouf (who is Lebanese) tells about the Polish Captain in London during World War II. He picked up a street walker and took her out to dinner. They went back to her apartment and had a wonderful evening.

Next morning she fixed him breakfast, helped him on with his boots, and as he walked out the door, she shouted, "Hey, dearie! What about money?"

"Madam!" said the Captain with a flourish. "A Polish officer never accepts money!"

* * *

How do Polacks reproduce?

They exchange underwear.

* * *

A Polish girl was walking down Main Street with a pig under her arm. She met a girl friend who said, "Where did you get the pig?"

And the pig said, "I won her in a raffle!"

*   *   *

Miami attorney Arthur Davis likes the one about the Pole whose wife had just given birth. When the nurse brought the news, he took it very casually. She decided to shake him up a bit and brought a black baby.

"What do you think of your new son?" she asked.

"Cute little cheeks," replied the new father. "Tight hair! Real nice!"

"Aren't you surprised that it's black?" questioned the astonished nurse.

"Heck no!" said the Polack. "My wife burn everything!"

*   *   *

Have you heard about the new Polish underarm deodorant?

It's called: No Bugs My Lady.

*   *   *

What happens when you give a Polish hooker a quarter?

You get double green stamps and twenty-four cents change.

* * *

Lloyd Gaynes, ABC-TV West Coast director of daytime programming, tells about the Polish couple in a motel. A sex maniac crashed into their room and at gunpoint forced the husband out of bed.

He drew a circle on the floor with a piece of chalk, and then said to him, "Stand in that circle. If you move out of it, I'll kill you!"

The intruder hopped in bed with the Pole's wife, made love to her for over an hour and then left. "My god!" cried the distraught woman. "Why didn't you do something?"

"I did," said the Polack. "I jumped out of the circle three times!"

* * *

What's the difference between a Polish wedding and a Polish funeral?

One less drunk.

* * *

Polish Lipstick: Preparation H.

* * *

A Polish couple got married and on their wedding night checked into a motel. They got themselves settled and in a few moments she called, "How about it, Chet?"

There was no answer. An hour later she repeated the question: "Chet, how about it?"

Still no answer. Soon it got to be five in the morning and by then she was fuming. "Chet, how about it?"

Finally he answered, "How about what?"

"How about going to sleep?" she replied.

* * *

Why don't Polish mothers like to breast-feed their children?

It hurts too much when they boil their nipples.

* * *

What do they call a Polish prostitute?

A ski jump.

* * *

TV Director Bill Darcy tells about the groom at a Polish wedding. The ceremony had taken place in the ballroom of the town hotel. The newly married husband came down from the bridal suite and said to a buddy, "My best friend be upstairs in bed with my wife!"

"What are you going to do about it?" asked his pal.

"Nothing," replied the Polack. "He so drunk he thinks he be me!"

*   *   *

Novack: I came home yesterday and found stranger making love to my wife.
Cusick: What you do?
Novack: I fix him. I threw his umbrella out window and pray for rain.

*   *   *

Why did the bride think she had the most posh Polish wedding in Poland?

Her veil practically covered her overalls.

*   *   *

Witkowski got into the mine elevator, chuckling out loud.

"What's the joke?" asked the foreman.

"I sure have big laugh on Jancywicz," replied the Polack. "I just find out he pay my wife five dollars to kiss her and I do it for nothing!"

*   *   *

Miss Luzinski was driving along the highway when a police car stopped her. The cop said, "Why don't you have a red light on this car?"

"It ain't that kind of a car!" she answered with a smile.

*   *   *

Television and motion picture scribe, Brad Radnitz, tells about the girl who, against her family's wishes, ran off and married a Polack. The eloping bride received the following telegram from her parents:

"DO *NOT* COME HOME AND ALL WILL BE FORGIVEN."

*   *   *

Miss Kozcynski sat opposite a man on a desolate train, looking sad and lonely. He read his magazines for awhile and then said, "Excuse me, Miss! Would you like to take a look at my *Cosmopolitan?*"

"Mister!" said the Polish girl. "If you dare try, I'll scream!"

*   *   *

Middle-aged Wojeck and Rojeck were sitting in a saloon discussing their past lives. "I've lived a good life." said Wojeck. "There's only one thing I could be ashamed of. My mother once caught me in a very embarrassing act!"

"Don't worry about it," soothed Rojeck. "All us kids did that!"

"I know," said Wojeck. "But it was only yesterday that she caught me!"

*   *   *

Why do Polish women wear veils when they get married?

To keep the flies off their faces.

*   *   *

Novack: I come home last night and find some strange guy kissing my wife.

Cusick: Holy smoke! What you do?

Novack: Ha! Ha! I fix them. I shut off lights so they not see what they were doing.

* * *

Comedy Writer Ray Parker tells about the Polish teenagers who came home from their honeymoon. The next day the bridegroom found his wife in the kitchen crying.

"What's the matter, honey?" he inquired.

"I rinsed the ice cubes in this hot water and now I can't find them," she explained tearfully.

* * *

Sophie: I never met you before but I've heard plenty about your lovemaking.
Zeke: Oh, it be nothing.
Sophie: That's what I heard.

* * *

Prisoner Pozinski serving a twenty-year sentence in a Michigan jail was reminiscing with a fellow inmate about his wife.

"We used to have such fun at the seaside burying each other in the soft, white sand!"

"Must've been nice!" said his cellmate.

"Yeah," said the Polack, "When I get out, I think I go back and dig her up!"

* * *

Adam and Eve must have been the first Polacks. They didn't have any clothes, all they had to eat was an apple, and they thought they were living in Paradise.

* * *

Drakich and Wishnak are sipping a beer at the neighborhood gin mill. "What have you be doing today?" asked Drakich.

"I be laying linoleum," replied Wishnak.

"Has she got a friend?" said Drakich.

* * *

Polish Love Song: "She was going to have her face lifted but she didn't have the Jack."

* * *

Witkowski suspected his wife of cheating. One day he rushed into the apartment unexpectedly and shot the two occupants dead. Then he looked around and said, "Hey, this is the wrong apartment."

* * *

Kazewski and Giordano agreed to a bet on who could make love to his wife more times in one night. They took adjoining hotel rooms and decided that each time they did they would carve a notch on the wall.

Giordano performed once at ten o'clock, placing a scratch on the wall. Then at two A.M. he drew another gash. By six o'clock he had three scratches.

At eight in the morning, the Polack came in and looked at the marks. "My god! One hundred and eleven!" cried Kazewski. "He beat me by three!"

* * *

Giant Polish dock worker, Kraczewski, was considered by most of the longshore-men to be a great lover. They claimed he could make love to twenty girls in an hour. When some disbelieving seamen showed up, bets were made, and the next night twenty girls were lined up in one of the warehouses.

The big Polack went to work. He made love to the first dozen, when suddenly he fell to the floor in a state of exhaustion.

His pals rushed up to him, screaming, "What happened?"

"I dunno," answered Kraczewski. "I did okay this afternoon at rehearsal!"

*　　*　　*

Farmers Dumbrowski and Kadlubek met in town:

Dumbrowski: I'm married twenty-five year today.

Kadlubek: Congratulations!

Dumbrowski: What you think? My wife told me to kill a chicken to celebrate, but I didn't.

Kadlubek: How come?

Dumbrowski: Why take it out on a chicken for something that happened twenty-five years ago.

KOLACHKI

What do you get when you cross a midget with a Polack?

A short garbage man.

*   *   *

"Do you know how to save a Polack?"

"No!"

"That's good!"

*   *   *

Brain Tumor: Pimple on a Polack's behind.

*   *   *

Dave Traurig, Sales Director for the Sheraton Hotels and motor inns, tells about Sladowski and Wiznecki getting a job in a factory. The first day there, Wiznecki climbed up on a ladder, stretched out his arms and shouted: "I'm a light! I'm a light!"

"What the hell are you doing?" asked the boss.

"I'm a light!" answered Wiznecki.

"Get down from there!" ordered the owner. "Do that again and you're fired!"

Soon as he walked away Wiznecki got up on the ladder again and with outstretched arms exclaimed: "I'm a light! I'm a light!"

"Okay, you're fired!" declared his employer.

The Pole started walking out of the plant when his friend, Sladowski, joined him. "Where the hell are you going?" asked the bewildered boss.

"I'm leaving!" replied the Polack indignantly. "I no work in place where there no be lights!"

*   *   *

And what about the Polack who hijacked a train to Cuba?

*   *   *

How to Tie Your Shoes—the Polish Way

What does X X X stand for?

Three Polacks co-signing a note.

*　　*　　*

Polish Car Pool: Eight Polacks carrying a Volkswagen to work.

*　　*　　*

Barbi McCulloch tells about the Polack and the two Mexicans who were to be hung in Texas for rustling. The lynch mob brought the three men to a tree at the edge of the Rio Grande. The idea was that after each man died, they'd cut the rope and he'd drift down the river out of sight.

They put the first Mexican in the noose, but he was so greasy he slipped out, fell into the river, and swam away to freedom.

They tied the noose around the second Mexican's head. He, too, oozed out of the rope, dropped into the river and escaped.

Then as they dragged the Polack toward the scaffold he said: "Could you make the noose a little tighter—I can't swim!"

*　　*　　*

Mort Fleischmann, RCA's West Coast director of news and information, contributed this gem:

Ziwacki bought a new car and after he left the showroom decided to catch a movie. When he came out, Ziwacki noticed he'd locked the car and left the keys in the ignition.

Ziwacki telephoned the dealer. "Which is cheapest window to break?"

"You don't have to break any of the windows," explained the auto seller. "I'll come right down with another key and we can open it together!"

"No! No!" shouted the Polack. "I got to know right now. It be going to rain and I want to put top up!"

*   *   *

"We must have done something to offend Mrs. Polanski, our neighbor," said Mrs. Brown to her husband. "She hasn't been over for several days."

"Be sure to find out what it is when she does come over," said Mr. Brown, "so we can do it again!"

*   *   *

Vocal groups booker Bonnie Larson tells about Dumbrowski and Moronski, who are out hunting and kill a deer. They each grabbed a hind leg and began pulling it toward their truck. But the antlers kept slowing them down.

Another hunter, passing by, said, "Why don't you pull that thing by the horns!" They did.

Two hours later, Dumbrowski said, "This be good idea. It be lot easier!"

"Yeah," said Moronski. "But we be getting further and further away from the truck!"

*   *   *

What did the Polish airplane manufacturers do before the airplane was invented?

They made parachutes.

*   *   *

How do you get a Polack out of a tub of water?

Throw in a bar of soap.

*   *   *

Miami philosopher Sid Danoff likes the one about the two Polacks who buy a truckload of watermelons for a buck apiece.

They sell every one of them for a dollar each. After counting up their money they realize they've got the same amount they spent.

"See," said one of the Polacks, "I told you we shoulda got a bigger truck!"

*   *   *

How did the Polack spell "farm"?

"E yi e yi yo."

*   *   *

What is the Polish national anthem?

Hymn to the Roto Rooter man.

*   *   *

What does it mean when you see an orange sewer plate on the street?

A Polish Howard Johnson's.

*   *   *

They just announced for the first time in history a new medical development in Poland. They performed the first transplant of a human appendix.

*   *   *

Dana Blatt of Encino asks: Why do Polacks make the best astronauts?

Because they took up space in school.

*   *   *

What do we do with our old sanitation trucks?

We send them to Poland and sell them as used campers.

*   *   *

Comedian-actor-writer Howard Storm came up with this pearl: What do goods made in Poland have stamped on them?

Untouched by human hands.

*   *   *

Why do Polacks make bad sky divers?

They miss the earth.

*   *   *

What happened to the Polish polo team?

The horses drowned.

*   *   *

Dave Levin, the storytelling sandwich sculptor of Art's Delicatessen in Studio City, entertains customers with this one: What did the Polish prostitute give her daughter for a birthday present?

Everything west of Broadway.

*   *   *

Poles indignant over the rash of jokes degrading every aspect of their culture, decided to prove to the world that they could make a significant contribution to society. They held a beauty contest in Poland. Nobody won.

*   *   *

Why don't you ever hear about Polacks committing suicide?

They can't get killed jumping out of a basement window!

*   *   *

Why do they only have two pallbearers at a Polish funeral?

Because a garbage can only has two handles.

What is a Polish seven-course dinner?

A pound of baloney and a six-pack.

* * *

Why are there more Blacks in Chicago than Poles in Detroit?

Chicago had first choice.

* * *

Definition Of a Maniac: A Polack in a bawdy house with a credit card.

* * *

Marie Ferrell of New Jersey says she felt awful when the American track team showed up late for their event at the Munich Olympics. The boys didn't know their starting time had been changed. But what about the poor Polish team. They showed up in Mexico City.

* * *

Sid Weksler, California frozen egg king, asks: Why does it take a Polack five days to wash his basement windows?

He needs four and a half days to dig the holes for the ladder.

*   *   *

Professor Potacki conducted an experiment to show how a frog reacted to human stimulus. The scientist explained: "At first the frog jumped sixteen feet. When I cut off one leg, I established that a three-legged frog could only jump twelve feet. I cut off another leg and yelled, 'Jump!' I concluded that a two-legged frog could only jump nine feet!"

"I then found that the frog with one leg could jump only six feet. I cut off the last leg, shouted 'Jump!' and the frog didn't move. So therefore I concluded that a frog with no legs is deaf!"

*   *   *

Who was Alexander Graham Polowski?

The first telephone Pole.

*   *   *

Custak walked into a lumber camp in Oregon and said to the man in charge, "I want to cut wood with you guys here in the north woods!" "You're nuts!" said the head lumberjack. "You're only five feet tall. You don't weigh more than a hundred pounds, soaking-wet. Besides, what kind of experience do you have to be a lumberjack?"

"The Sahara Forest!" replied the bold Polack.

*   *   *

UCLA co-ed Libby Getz asks: What is the *second* stupidest thing in the world?

A Polack out in the middle of the ocean, trying to build a foundation for a house.

*   *   *

What is the *stupidest* thing in the world?

An Italian trying to build a house on the foundation.

*   *   *

What is the easiest job in Poland?

Intelligence officer in the Polish army.

*   *   *

102

In what section of the newspaper do they print Polish obituaries?

Under *Civic Improvements*.

*   *   *

There is a contest that has $2.00 for the first prize. The second prize is a trip to Poland.

*   *   *

A tux-clad comedian, performing at Gene Penoz' Moose Club in Pittsburgh, was stunned momentarily after he asked: "What's black and white and floats down the river on its back?"

"The next comedian who tells a Polish joke," shouted a member of the audience.

*   *   *

What do you get when you cross a Polack and a flower?

A blooming idiot.

*   *   *

If there are thirty motorcycles going down the street, how can you tell which one the Polack is on ?

It's the one with the training wheels.

*   *   *

Russia claims they could have the world's largest zoo. All they have to do is build a fence around Poland.

*   *   *

What's the first thing a Polack does when he gets out of the shower?

Takes off his clothes.

*   *   *

Harry and Fred had been playing golf for twenty-five years and for twenty-five years Fred had lost to his pal. Fred decided to find the greatest partner to help him beat Harry. So he got this giant Polish steelworker.

They were out on the first tee, the hole was 501 yards. The Polack hit a tremendous drive and the ball landed on the green —a 501-yard smash.

"I can't beat this guy," moaned Harry. "He'll probably go two on every hole. Here's the money. Incidentally, how does he putt?"

"Same way he drives," said Fred, walking toward the club house.

*   *   *

Why do Polish men have pierced elbows?

So they can wear cuff links in the summer!

*   *   *

How do you know when a Polack has died?

All the garbage trucks have their lights on.

*   *   *

Singing star, Burt Taylor, tells about Polski at the airport trying to get back to Poland. The ticket cost $200. He only had $199.95. The Pole ran around stopping people to scrape up the nickel.

Finally, he cornered a well-dressed business executive and said, "Mister, you lend me nickel?"

"Leave me alone," said the man.

"Please," begged Polski. "I need five cents to go back to Poland."

"Oh, here's a quarter, then," said the man, "Take four more with you!"

*   *   *

For years the Russians have maintained that they invented almost every gadget or mechanical device known to man.

Though most of their claims have been disputed, even the Russians are willing to admit that the Polacks invented the limbo dance.

It came about quite by accident. They were trying to squeeze under the door of a pay toilet.

*   *   *

On the UCLA campus, Mike Bols tells about Karpinski trying to join a fraternity up at Washington State. The boys didn't want him. They told him in order to be accepted, he'd have to do three things: Drink a gallon of homemade liquor, kill a grizzly bear and rape an Eskimo woman.

The Polish student guzzled down the booze and then staggered off into the woods. He returned the next day, his clothes tattered and torn. "What happened?" asked the frat brothers.

"Never mind!" retorted the boy. "Where's that Eskimo woman you want me to kill!"

*   *   *

What do they call a pig in a blanket?

A Polish prostitute.

*   *   *

Mack: Do you know how to speak Polish?
Jack: No!
Mack: How does it feel to be dumber than a Polack?

*   *   *

What do they call a Polack who sits in a tree?

A branch manager.

*   *   *

Larry Yeston, Lerner shops exec, recalls the one about the Negro jumping up and down on a manhole cover, shouting, "49! 49! 49!"

107

Along came Kuloc. "What you do?" he said.

"Here man," said the Black, "you jump for awhile!"

Kuloc began leaping up and down on the manhole cover. Suddenly, the Black snatched the cover away and the Polack fell into the sewer.

The colored man replaced it and, jumping up and down, shouted, "50! 50! 50!"

* * *

Who wears a polka dot tie, an outrageously striped vest and checkered pants, and sits on a wall?

Humpty Dumbrowski.

* * *

Sharalee Beard, with the Johnny Mann Singers, tells about the man who walked into a cannibal butcher shop to buy a pound of brains. There were three piles. $1 a pound, $10 a pound, and $10,000 a pound.

"Why is the first pile only a dollar?" asked the customer.

"Those are white people's brains!" answered the cannibal proprietor.

"How come the second bunch is $10?"

"Those are Negro brains," said the owner.

"Why is the other pile $10,000?"

"They're Polish brains!" explained the boss.

"But why are they so expensive?"

"Do you know how many Polacks we have to kill to get a pound of brains!"

*   *   *

In Las Vegas, TV's Don Adams tells about the Indian (from Bombay), the Jew, and the Polack, who are stuck out in the country in a storm. They came to a farm house and asked to be put up for the night.

"I have a small cabin in back, but there's only room for two," said the farmer. "One of you will have to sleep in the barn."

The Indian volunteered. Five minutes later, he knocked on the cabin door and said to his Polish and Jewish friends, "I can't stay in the barn. There is a cow there and that is against my religion."

"That's all right," said the Jew. "I'll sleep in the barn."

Five minutes later, there was knock on the cabin door and the Jew said, "I'm sorry, there's a pig in the barn. That's against my religion."

109

"That's okay," said the Polack. "I'll sleep in the barn!"

Five minutes later, there was a knock on the door. The Indian and the Jew opened it and there stood the pig and the cow.

* * *

How many Polacks does it take to pull off a kidnapping?

Six.
One to kidnap the victim and five to write the ransom note.

* * *

Little Davie Blumenfield from Atlantic City asks: What's a Polish pencil?

A pencil with an eraser on both ends.

* * *

What's a Polish Mai-Tai?

Eight Polacks standing around drinking through straws from a septic tank.

* * *

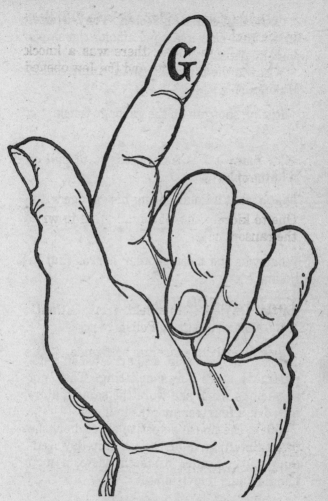

Polish Handkerhief, Monogrammed

Comedian-cruise director, Tony Noice, writes that this is a howl among the ship's passengers:

What is the toughest job in Hamtramck, Michigan?

Riding shotgun on the garbage truck.

*   *   *

What's a Garachski?

That's what a Polack opens his garage with.

*   *   *

What was the most popular horror film in Poland?

"*The Unsmellable Man.*"

*   *   *

Miss Pontiatowski was arrested in a department store for shoplifting. They got suspicious when she wore the same maternity dress fourteen months in a row.

When the house detective shook her, she immediately gave birth to a drip-dry wedding gown, a tube of tooth paste, a mop handle and a television set.

*   *   *

Real Estate Broker Jackie Peters tells about Kachowski and Wlasowich getting drunk and stumbling into an Irish wake. They were so polluted they couldn't even find the corpse. But for ten minutes they stood in front of a grand piano.

Finally, Kachowski nudged his friend and said, "Do you recognize him?"

"Hell, no!" slobbered Wlasowich. "But he sure has a great set of teeth!"

* * *

During a recent stock market dip, a broker lost everything. "I have no money to pay you, Mr. Kluzewski," he said to the plumber, who had just presented a large bill. "In lieu of payment will you take a Rembrandt?"

"If it has four good tires," said the Polack, "you got a deal!"

* * *

How can you tell a Polack from a monkey?

The monkey peels the banana before eating it.

* * *

Who has a beard, wears a dirty white robe
and rides a pig?

Lawrence of Poland.

Ted Sawaski, Rialto, California, insurance agent, tells about Stanislaw Putsidwakim going to court to have his name changed.

"I can understand how you feel," sympathized the judge. "A name like Stanislaw Putsidwakim could certainly be a handicap. What would you like to change it to?"

"*George* Putsidwakim," said the Polack.

*　　*　　*

One night on his TV show Joey Bishop broke up the audience with: "The other day I was in a town so small the head of the Mafia was Polish."

*　　*　　*

Why is a Polish postman like an ape?

Cause his feet smell like the inside of a gorilla's stomach.

*　　*　　*

They put an Indian on a nickel—now they're going to put a Polack on a slug.

*　　*　　*

Stanley and his girl friend were sitting in the park. Suddenly, a police car whizzed by with its siren going full blast. "Listen, darling," cooed the girl, "they're playing our song!"

* * *

Wiznecki got an out of town construction job and asked his pal, Boleslaw, to check up on his wife to see that she didn't fool around with anybody.

Six months later he returned and found his spouse and his buddy in bed doing the very thing he tried to avoid. Wiznecki called his wife every name in the book and then threatened divorce.

"And as for you, you dirty dog," the Polack shouted at his best friend, "couldn't you at least stop while I'm talking to you!"

* * *

Polish girl received a letter from her boyfriend in the army with a bunch of Xs on the bottom. "The dirty rat," she muttered. "I'll teach him to double-cross me!"

* * *

117

Polish Proverb: If ignorance was commercial we'd all be millionaires.

* * *

Bob Feldman of Acme Vending likes the one about the Pole, the Black, and the Mexican, who were out of work and living together. The Polack came home one night and announced he had gotten a job. "Hey, fellas, wake me up tomorrow morning at six," he said, "I have to be at work by 6:30!"

While the Polack slept, the Black said to the Mexican, "He got a job because he's white. We can't get one because we're brown and black." So during the night they put shoe black all over the Polack. Then they agreed to wake him late.

Next morning, when the Polish boy arrived at work, the foreman said, "Who are you?"

"You hired me yesterday," he replied. "You told me to be here at 6:30!"

"I hired a white man—you're black."

"I am not!"

"Yes you are! Go look in the mirror!"

The Polack rushed over to a mirror, looked at himself and exclaimed, "My God! They woke up the wrong one!"

* * *

Wysotski and Voytek went to a lumber yard. Wysotski waited in the car while Voytek spoke to the foreman. "I want some 3x4's!" said Voytek.

"We've only got 2x4's!" said the lumber man.

"Wait, I go ask my partner!" Voytek returned and said "Okay."

"How long do you want them?" asked the foreman.

"Just a minute, I go check with my partner!" Voytek came back in a few seconds and said, "We'll want them for awhile —we building a house!"

*   *   *

Do you know how Polacks make babies?

No.
Boy, are you dumb!

*   *   *

Why do Polacks wear turtleneck sweaters?

To hide their flea collars.

*   *   *

Zaleski and Gornicki were riding in the country when their car broke down.

"How far is it back to Detroit?" asked Zaleski of a service station attendant.

"Twenty miles," he replied.

"We'd better get going," said Gornicki. "Twenty miles is a long way to walk!"

"That's not so much!" answered Zaleski. "It's only ten miles a piece!"

*   *   *

"What you doin'?" asked Ladislas.

"I write letter to myself," answered Sigismund.

"What you tell yourself?"

"How do I know?" snapped Sigismund. "I no get letter until tomorrow!"

*   *   *

Wojawicz and Slovak were placed in a padded cell. Wojawicz kept trying to hammer a nail into the wall. But he had the head of the nail against the wall and was hammering on the pointed end.

"I'm supposed to be nuts," he says to his friend, "but the nails they give you here have the pointed end on the wrong side."

"You're crazy, all right," says Slovak. "That nail is for the other wall!"

*   *   *

Zuchva and Koszyczki lived together, and one night Zuchva came home and found Koszyczki walking around the apartment without any clothes on except for a high top hat.

"Why you walk around house without clothes on?" asked Zuchva.

"It make no difference," answered Koszyczki. "Nobody ever come here to see us."

"Then why you wear high top hat?"

"Somebody might!"

*　　*　　*

THE END ...

of the Polish jokes, that is. Please turn the book over and start all over again, to read the Italian jokes. (Unless you're Polish, of course, in which case you merely have to stand on your head.)

NOTE

If you are Polish and find it
difficult to laugh at yourself or
if you have become angry,
there is one way to have a laugh and
lessen your anger. Follow these
instructions carefully: (1) Every
time you see the word *Polish*
(or any slang meaning same) substitute
one of the following words:
Jewish, Irish, Chinese, German, British,
Icelandic, Brazilian, Canadian, Filipino, Hungarian,
Egyptian, Russian, Australian, Norwegian,
African, Korean, Gypsy, Afghanistanian,
etc. See how easy it is to be funny!
(2) Now you can read the Italian jokes.
P.S. ... heard any good Jewish or Irish
jokes lately? We're doing another book,
and this time it's *their* turn.

HOORAY

FOR THE

POLES!

(an unpaid political advertisement)

THE CRITICS APPROVE!

I reada dis book ina one night. Summa the words is hard, but the pikshas helpa. Alla da udda groups is a gonna to be jealous, but weva been waiting afor to be recognized alonga time. Now isa time! Here it is! Alla da greatness ofa da Italians. I laffa so hard my belly hertz. Dem Polak jokes don'ta maka much sense, but whadda you expect? My brother-in-law isa a Pole, and he don't either. Buy it quick! Giva one to your mama. She lika it too.

—Guiseppe De Stefano, Book Reviewer
The Salinas Italo-American Blade

THE OFFICIAL POLISH-ITALIAN JOKEBOOK

compiled and edited by
Larry Wilde

illustrations by
Ron Wing

PINNACLE BOOKS • NEW YORK CITY

THE OFFICIAL ITALIAN JOKEBOOK

ANTIPASTO

Do you consider an I.Q. of 144 high?

Yes!
For twelve Italians?

* * *

When are the three times an Italian sees his priest?

When he is born!
When he is married!
And when he is electrocuted!

* * *

Do you know why Polish jokes are so short?

So Italians can understand them.

* * *

What do they call an Italian submarine captain?

Chicken of the sea.

* * *

How do you get 100 Italians into one square inch?

Put a penny in it!

* * *

TV director Don Pietro tells about Rizzo and Martinelli being torpedoed during World War II. They managed to save themselves on a life raft.

Suddenly, Rizzo noticed a periscope skimming the water. He nudged his comrade and said, "Hey, is that a U-boat?

"No!" said Rizzo, seeing the periscope. "That's a no my boat!"

* * *

Why do Italians paint their trash cans orange and blue?

So their mothers will think they're going to Howard Johnson's.

* * *

What is the thinnest book in the world?
The History Of Italian War Heroes.

* * *

And: *Polish Royalty.*

* * *

And: *Who's Who In Poland.*

* * *

What is the difference between an Italian mother-in-law and an elephant?

About fifty pounds.

* * *

California's indefatigable charity drives chairlady, Basie McCulloch, tells about Ferrara the Flyer during World War II. He'd never shot down a British plane and everybody in the squadron kidded him about it.

One day while on patrol Ferrara spotted five British transport planes. He zipped into their formation and shot down all five.

Now he couldn't wait to tell his fellow

pilots. Ferrara landed quickly, jumped out of his plane and rushed over to a colonel standing beside a map table.

"I justa shoot down five a British a transports!" shouted the proud Italian.

"I say, bad luck, old chap!" replied the officer.

*   *   *

How can the police tell when a house has been burglarized by an Italian?

When the toilet seat is up and the cat is pregnant.

*   *   *

Socialite Edie Bato from England tells about Rizzuto and Santini having lunch. "Say, Santini, do you likea bigga fat woman with a long a straggly hair?" "No," said his friend.

"You like a woman with a garlic come a from her mouth alla the time?" "No!" said Santini.

"You like a woman with a big, thick a hips and a varicose a veins!" "No!" answered his pal.

"Then how come," shouted Rizzuto, "you make a love a to my wife?"

*   *   *

Where do the Italians go for a big night out?

The corner cesspool.

* * *

Why doesn't an Italian shave on weekends?

Because his razor sleeps late.

* * *

An Englishman, a Frenchman, and an Italian were captured during World War II and brought to a prison camp. "How many pairs of underwear do you need?" asked the quartermaster.

"Seven!" said the Englishman. "A pair for each day of the week!"

"Four!" said the Frenchman. "One for each week in the month!"

"And what about you?" inquired the sergeant of the Italian. "How many pairs of underwear do you need?"

"Twelve!" replied the Italian.

"What the hell do you need twelve for?"

"One a for January, one a for February, one a...."

* * *

Fred Holliday, host of ABC's "The Girl In My Life," tells about the two men standing on a street corner. "I can't stand Eyetalians," said one man. "I hate 'em! They turn my stomach!"

Just then an organ grinder and his monkey came by. The angry man gave the monkey a quarter.

"Why'd you do that?" asked his friend. "I thought you hated Italians!"

"Yeah," said the other man. "But they're so cute when they're little!"

Why don't Italians play hide and seek?

Because nobody will go look for them.

* * *

Why don't they kill flies in Italy?

Cause it's the national bird.

* * *

What's the easiest way to spot an Italian ship?

When it's put on water—it sinks.

* * *

Motion picture director Vern Zimmermann likes the one about the night Mrs. Mantoni got into a taxi. After riding awhile, she realized she'd forgotten her pocketbook and had no money to pay the fare. The meter now read $7.00.

"Mista driver," she cried. "You betta stop. I no canna pay you!"

"Oh, that's all right," said the cabbie. "I'll just pull down a dark street, get in

the back seat with you, take off your panties. . . ."

"Mista, you gonna get gypped," said the Italian lady. "My panties only cost a 49 cents!"

*   *   *

If an Italian drowns, how do they locate the body?

By the oil slick.

*   *   *

What is an Italian cookout?

A fire in a garbage can.

*   *   *

How can you tell an Italian airplane?

It's the one with hair under the wings.

*   *   *

How do you break an Italian's finger?

You punch him in the nose.

*   *   *

How do you take an Italian census?

Count the basement windows and multiply by ten.

* * *

What do they call an Italian girl who keeps running away from home?

A virgin.

* * *

How would you get twenty-eight Italians in a Volkswagen?

Throw a dime in the back seat.

* * *

Why do flies have wings?

So they can beat Italians to the garbage can.

* * *

What do you call an Italian who marries a Negro?

A social climber.

* * *

What do you get when you cross an Italian with an ape?

A retarded ape.

*   *   *

Why do Italians wear shoes with sharp pointed toes?

So they can kill the roaches that retreat into the corners.

*   *   *

Fellow dies and is met by Saint Peter at the Pearly Gates. "Before you can get in you must spend six months in Hell! You have a choice. Either the regular Hell or the Italian Hell!"

"What's the difference?" asked the fellow.

"In the regular Hell," explained Saint Peter, "they tie you to a stake, pour gasoline over you, strike the match and you burn for twelve hours and then you rest for twelve hours."

"And the Italian Hell?"

"They tie you to a stake, pour gasoline over you, set you on fire and you burn for twelve hours and then rest for twelve hours."

17

"But I don't see the difference!" said the man.

"If I were you," advised Saint Peter, "I'd take the Italian Hell. Somebody usually forgets the matches or the gasoline...."

* * *

For Sale

10,000 genuine Italian army rifles. Cheap. Have never been fired. Have only been used once.

* * *

How did God make an Italian?

He took some clay in each hand and threw it together ... Wop!

* * *

How would you describe six Italians in a circle?

A dope ring.

* * *

What do you have when you find twelve Italians on your front lawn?

Fertilizer.

* * *

How do you keep your Italian servant from going into the liquor closet?

Hide the key under the soap.

* * *

What happens when an Italian housewife doesn't pay her garbage bill?

They don't bring her any more.

* * *

How can you recognize an Italian helicopter?

The small blade goes: Guinea, Guinea, Guinea!!!! And the big blade goes: Wop! Wop! Wop!!!!

* * *

19

What would be a good description of 250 Italian paratroopers?

Air Pollution.

*   *   *

Why did Mussolini have six bullets in him when he was found dead?

Because 200 Italian sharpshooters were firing at him.

*   *   *

Concord Fabrics exec, Morris Resner, sent this along: three astronauts, a Russian, an American and an Italian were discussing outer space. "There is no doubt in our minds," declared the Russian, "that we will be the first ones to land on Mars."

"No way," interrupted the American. "We've been on the moon 14 times and *we're* going to be first on Mars."

"Well, you fellas canna fight alla you want over landing onna Mars," challenged the Italian. "We gonna be the firsta to land on the sun!"

"Don't be ridiculous!" said the American. You can't land on the sun. It's too hot!"

Italian Firing Squad

"Aha, you think we a stupid or something?" answered the Italian. "We know that! We gonna land at a night!"

* * *

Do you know why Italians can't surf?

Cause they're wop-sided.

* * *

TV commercials producer, Chuck Stuart, regales members of The Sanctuary—Anne Marie Bennstrom's hip Hollywood health spa—with this pearl:

An army sergeant told Private Palumbo to go to the end of the line. He did, but then returned. "I thought I told you to go to the end of the line," barked the NCO. "Why did you come back?"

"Because there's somebody already there!" explained the Italian.

* * *

What's the last thing they do at an Italian wedding?

Flush the punch bowl.

* * *

New Italian Army Tank:
    Four gears in reverse.
    One forward. In case the enemy gets
    behind them.

*   *   *

How does an Italian housewife reply when
the sanitation men ask, "Any garbage
today?"

"Yes," she says, "I'll take three bags!"

*   *   *

What is the simplest mechanical operation
in the world?

An Italian!
There are only two moving parts—his bottom and his mouth—and they are inter-
changeable.

*   *   *

Chico: I'm a nobody's fool.
Carlo: Maybe somebody'll adopta you.

*   *   *

How do you train Italians to be soldiers?

First teach them to raise their hands above their heads.

At a Mafia party how can you tell the guest of honor?

He's the one with the brand-new cement overcoat.

*　　*　　*

Marti Jones of Parsons, Kansas, points out that all American ships have "U S S" in front of their names. Ships of the British navy are preceded by "H. M. S." Italian ships are prefaced by the letters: "A M B." Atsa my boat.

*　　*　　*

Why does time go so fast in Italy?

Because every time you look around another Dago's by?

*　　*　　*

What is the best way to grease a Ferrari?

Run over an Italian.

*　　*　　*

Salesman Tom Boyd tells his customers about Valenti and Costanza, who are out in a row boat, fishing. Suddenly, Valenti lands a big one and remarks to his friend, "This is a some place to fish. How we gonna remember it!" Costanza immediately jumps overboard and disappears beneath the surface.

In a moment he climbs back on board. "What did you do?" asked Valenti.

"So we can remember this a spot," answered Costanza, "I painted an X on the bottom of a the boat!"

"Boy, you musta be stupid or something!" berated Valenti. "What a we gonna do if next time we donna get the same a boat!"

*　　*　　*

At an Italian wedding how can you tell the difference between members of the Mafia and the musicians?

The musicians are the ones without the violin cases.

*　　*　　*

How do they separate the men from the boys in the Italian navy?

With crowbars.

*   *   *

Sherry Hinderstein of Brooklyn tells about the time Michelangelo was painting the ceiling of the Cistine Chapel. He was getting tired lying on his back and in rolling over noticed that an Italian woman was praying down in the chapel. The great artist decided to play a little prank.

He sat at the edge of the scaffold and shouted: "I am Jesus Christ! I am Jesus Christ! Listen to me and I will perform miracles!"

The Italian lady looked up, clasping her rosary and answered back: "Shut upa your mouth! I'ma talka to your mother!"

*   *   *

News Item on Society Page:
Members of the Italian Suicide Squad will meet next week for their 28th Anniversary Reunion.

*   *   *

What's the only thing smaller than the Swiss navy?

The Italian air force.

* * *

Why can't an Italian take a shower?

Because oil and water don't mix.

* * *

What is every Italian's ambition?

To be rich enough to have a Polish gardener.

* * *

Why do so many Italian submarines sink?

The screen door's in the hull.

* * *

What do they call a good-looking Italian girl?

Lucky!

* * *

As an experiment, two scientists decided to mate a male human with a female gorilla. They agreed only someone really stupid would submit to such an act. So they went down to the docks and grabbed Manicotti, who had just gotten off the boat.

"We'll give you $5,000 to go to bed with a gorilla!" proposed one of the scientists. "Will you do it?"

"Okay, I do it!" agreed Manicotti. "But on three conditions!"

"What are they?" asked the men of science.

"Firsta, I'ma only gonna do it a once!" said the Italian. "Seconda, nobody canna watch. And a third, if a kid is a born, it's a gotta be raised a Catholic!"

* * *

Los Angeles accountant Ken Gerstenfeld forwarded this dilly told him by comedian-singer Steve Rossi: Three weeks after arriving in America Guiseppe telephoned his mother in Rome.

"Mama Mia!" he bellowed excitedly. "I'ma so happy. I'ma gonna marry ana Americana girl!"

"No! No!" pleaded his mother. "Ameri-

cana girl a no good. She's a bad a cook. She's a bad in a the bed. And if you have a the fight, she's a gon call you *wop!*"

Despite his mother's pleas Guiseppe married the girl and a month later again phoned his mother.

"Mama! Mama! You alla wrong!" Guiseppe exclaimed. "She's a great a cook! She's a wonderful inna the bed! And mama, the only time she's a call me *wop* is when I calla her *coon.*

PASTA

Two boyhood chums from Palermo immigrated to New York and resumed their friendship.

Tony: This is a some wonderful country. Where else coulda you walk down a the street, meet a complete a stranger, have a dinner with him, and then be invited to spend a the night at his house?

Patsy: This a happen to you?

Tony: To me, no—But it a happen to my sister.

*   *   *

What do two flamingos do when they get married?

They put two cast iron Italians out on their front lawn.

*   *   *

Comedy writer Danny Simon tells about the housewife who picked out three small tomatoes at Alfredo's Vegetable Market and was told they were seventy-five cents.

"Seventy-five cents for these tiny tomatoes?" she exclaimed. "Well, you can just take them and you know what you can do with them!"

"I can't a lady!" replied Alfredo. "There'sa ninety-five centa cucumber already a there!"

*　　*　　*

Tony: Every night I dream of a sign on a the door and I push and a push but I no canna open it.
Patsy: What does a da sign say?
Tony: Pull!

*　　*　　*

Nick Pensiero, RCA Director of Public Affairs, tells about Carmella who loved her husband Carmine. Carmine loved cheese. Carmine died. Carmella didn't believe in reincarnation but since Carmine loved cheese so much, she thought it'd be nice to line his coffin with every kind of cheese imaginable.

Carrying the casket down the aisle, the pallbearer on the back handle let go. "Why you do such a thing?" asked Carmella.

"If Carmine is able to do what I think he's a do," replied the man. "He's a able to walk!"

*   *   *

New Italian car called a "Fiasco." It uses no fuel. You just put Lasagna in the tank. Then Linguini with clam sauce and then some Ravioli Alla Marinara. By the time it gets to the engine it's pure gas.

*   *   *

What's an Italian virgin?

A girl who can run faster than her brother.

*   *   *

Tony: Why donna you wash your face? I canna see whata you had a for breakfast this morning.
Patsy: Okay, biga shotsa. What did I have?
Tony: Pizza.
Patsy: You wrong. That was a yesterday.

*   *   *

In the Middle East, during the Six-Day War, the Israelis attacked the Arabs and two hours later the Italian army surrendered.

Columbus was the first wheeler dealer. He didn't know where he was going. When he got there he didn't know where he was. When he got back he didn't know where he had been. And he did it all on borrowed money.

* * *

Francesca wrote to her boyfriend Gino in the army: "Thought you'd like to know that I haven't been sick for three months!"

Private Gino answered: "That's fine! We've all had the flu here!"

* * *

"Hey, Donatelli, you oughta pulla your shades down when you kiss your wife. I saw you last night!"

"Ha! Ha! The joke's onna you. I wasn't a home last night!"

* * *

Angelo came home quite drunk and his wife wouldn't let him in the house. "Hey, Pizzapuss," he shouted from below their window. "If you donna let me in, I'ma

gonna tell everybody I slepta with you before we got married."

"Go ahead," yelled back his wife. "And I'ma gonna tell them you weren't the firsta one!"

*　　*　　*

Rosa went to confession and told the priest that she had been having an affair with a man.

"But this is the sixth time you have told me about this," remonstrated the priest.

"Yes, I know, Father," said the woman. "I like to talk about it."

*　　*　　*

Carmela and Angelina were discussing their boss. "Aren't you just crazy about him," said Carmela. "He dresses so well!" "And so quickly too!" added Angelina.

*　　*　　*

Tony: You sitta in the park with a nice a girl. Whata you do?
Patsy: Buy her a baga peanuts?
Tony: No! You puta you arms around her

and your lips to hers. But she pusha you away. Then whata you do?

Patsy: I take backa my baga peanuts. . . .

* * *

Mrs. Compari meets Mrs. Sandelli at the butcher store. "I hear you husbanda hada monkey glands put in," said Mrs. Compari. "How's he doing?"

"I donna know!" answered Mrs. Sandelli. "He's a still up in a the chandelier eating peanuts."

* * *

"No man is so well known as he thinks he is," once said Enrico Caruso, the world-famed tenor.

"While driving through New York State, my car broke down and while it was being fixed I became friendly with a farmer who was getting gas. He asked me my name and I told him it was Caruso."

"The farmer shook my hand and said, 'Never thought I'd see a big man like you way out here in the country!' "

" 'Caruso!' he exclaimed. 'Wait till I tell my wife I met the great traveler, Robinson Caruso!' "

* * *

Exec Secretary, Beverly Kritchman, tells about the old Sicilians who were playing *bocce* and discussing the ideal way of dying. Cardoni, aged seventy-five, said, "Me, I likea to crash in a car going 100 miles an hour!"

Bronzini, aged eighty-five, said, "I like a to leave this a world in a plane a crash!"

Ronzoni, aged ninety-five, said, "Me, I'd likea to be shota by a jealous a husband!"

* * *

An American tenor was making his debut in *Pagliacci* at the La Scala Opera House in Milan. When he finished the exciting Vesta La Giuba, the audience applauded and an elderly man sitting down front stood up and exclaimed, "Sing it again!"

The tenor, delighted by the request, did an encore. The opera lover again leaped to his feet and implored "Sing it again!"

After five encores the tenor walked to the edge of the stage and said, "Thank you, for your very gracious reception!"

Once more the old man shouted, "Sing it again!"

"I'm sorry sir," begged the singer. "We must go on. I can't sing it again!"

"Yes," declared the opera fan. "You'll sing it again, until you sing it right!"

* * *

Tony: This is a very high class suit I'm a wearing. You never guess what I pay for it.

Patsy: $5.

Tony: Ah, that was justa lucky guess.

*   *   *

If you see a row of houses that all look alike, how can you tell which one is Italian?

It's the one with the diving board over the cesspool.

*   *   *

During World War II Hermann Goebbels rushed into Hitler's office and said, "We are having trouble with our sewage disposal. We need to have a larger processing plant."

"We can have the largest sewage processing plant in the world!" exclaimed the Fuhrer.

"How?" asked Goebbels.

"Just build a levee around Italy!" replied the German dictator.

*   *   *

Why did the Italian mother decide to have her baby in the drugstore?

Because they had free delivery service.

* * *

Accordion virtuoso, Tony Lavelli, tells about the perplexed wife talking to her angry husband: "Hey, Gino, what's a matta for you? Monday you like a lasagna; Tuesday you like a lasagna; Wednesday you like a lasagna. Now all of a sudden, here it is Thursday, and you no like a lasagna."

* * *

Pizza: A broiled manhole cover.

* * *

What is Italy's national fish?

They don't have one—it drowned.

* * *

Tony: How canna you be so stupid?
Patsy: Well, it ain'ta something you canna pick up over a night.

* * *

How can you tell a happy Italian motor-cyclist?

By the bugs on his teeth.

A famous Italian movie producer living in Beverly Hills brought his mother over from Genoa to live with him. Mama immediately took over all the cooking chores.

One day she telephoned Jorgensen's, the posh grocery emporium, to give them an order. "I want a quart of a milk, a dozen eggs, a few apples and an amatta!"

"I've got the milk, the eggs, and a few apples," said the clerk, checking the list, "but what's a matta?"

"Nothing's amatta wid me," replied the old lady. "What's amatta wid you?"

*   *   *

It is a common belief that all Italian women are enormously fat. Like all popular misconceptions there are examples to prove the opposite.

World traveler, Danny Desmond, says, "I met a girl in Rome who was so skinny, if she put a pizza on her head, she could've rented herself out as a beach umbrella."

*   *   *

Badly injured in an automobile accident, Gaspari had to have a brain transplant.

A team of surgeons put him under anesthesia, removed his brain and went into the next room to get the new one.

When they returned to the operating room, Gaspari was gone. The police searched everywhere for him, but to no avail. He had vanished. The doctors contacted Interpol and they checked throughout the world trying to find this poor Italian who had left the hospital without his brain.

Finally, five years later, he was found. Gaspari was teaching school in Poland.

*　*　*

Edwin Weinberger, producer-writer of "The Mary Tyler Moore Show," tells about the captain of an Al Italia jet who was speaking over the intercom to his passengers:

"Folksa, I got a some good news and a some bad news. Firsta, the bad news! We're lost!"

"Now the gooda news! We're a makinga excellent a time!"

*　*　*

47

Ten years after his arrival in America, Pasquale had saved enough money from his fruit and vegetable business to build a huge house.

"I wanna three bedrooms a upstairs," he explained to the builder. "I wanna large a living room with a nice a bigga staircase leading up to the bedroom. And right over here next to the staircase I wanna hollow statue."

Months later he returned and found everything built to his specifications. Then he noticed a statue next to the staircase.

"Hey, what's a matta wid you?" shouted Pasquale. "You no *capish* what I tella you!"

"Isn't that what you ordered?" Asked the builder. "A hollow statue?"

"Are you a stupe or something," cried the Italian. "I wanna one a those things that goes a ring-a-ring, you pick 'em up and say 'hallo, is tat choo?'"

*   *   *

How does an Italian Admiral review his fleet?

Through a glass-bottomed boat.

*   *   *

How do you sink an Italian submarine?
Put it in water.

*   *   *

Patsy: My daughter Rosa, she's a spend all her time with Socrates, Aristotle and a Plato.

Tony: Whatsa matta, she no like a the American a boys?

*   *   *

A well-heeled matron walked into Grimaldi's grocery store and said, "Do you keep brown sugar?"

"No, lady," replied the owner. "When it getsa dirty we throw it away."

*   *   *

The doctor came out of Rizzoli's bedroom and said to his wife, "Frankly, I don't like the way your husband looks at all!"

"I don't either," she said. "But he's nice to the kids."

*   *   *

Italy was finally ready to put a man in space. The only detail left was to select an astronaut. One hundred fifty of the finest army officers were selected and assembled under the balcony of the pope. His Holiness would make the final choice.

"One of you brave men will carry our flag into space," announced the supreme Catholic leader, looking down upon the throng of soldiers. "That man will have the distinction of leaving earth, to circle the globe and discover new worlds for mankind. Whoever this feather falls upon—he will be the lucky winner!"

The pope removed the feather from his hat, dropped it over the balcony and went back inside the Vatican. He never noticed that, as the feather floated downward, 150 men were inhaling huge gulps of air and blowing it upward.

Toward the end of World War II, when the Italians were fighting the Germans, the Nazi soldiers came up with a scheme to kill many of Mussolini's men.

They simply yelled, "Hey, Luigi!" When an Italian infantryman stuck his head up and answered, "Si?" Boom! He was dead.

That's all the Krauts did: "Luigi?" "Si?" Boom!

After thousands of Italians had been wiped out, they decided to retaliate. They figured that every German's name was Hans. So an Italian captain shouted, "Hey, Hans!"

Silence. "Hey, Hans!" he repeated.

"Is that you Luigi?"

"Si!"

Boom!

*   *   *

There's no way to prove it, but Al Capone was once quoted as saying: "I don't enjoy killing and robbing innocent people—but it keeps me out of trouble."

*   *   *

Have you heard about the new Italian birth control pill?

It's called Sulfa-Denial.

* * *

Lorenzo was extolling the virtues of his newly adopted homeland. "This isa greata country," he declared. "Looka at Sinatra. Where elsea could a piece of spaghetti wind upa with a so mucha gravy!"

* * *

Bologna and Maggio were hunting. They split up. Maggio heard rustling in the bushes and by mistake shot his friend. He tried to remove the bullet but when it became impossible, he carried Bologna to a doctor.

Two hours later, after the M.D. had patched up the wounded hunter, Maggio asked, "Please, how is my friend?"

"He'd be a hellava lot better," declared the M.D., "if you hadn't gutted him!"

* * *

Viggiani, Novelli and Columbo were out hunting when they came upon some tracks. After looking at them closely, Viggiani said, "Those are a bear tracks!"

"No! No!" disagreed Novelli. "Those are a deer tracks!"

"Hey, Columbo," they both asked, "whata you thinka they are?"

Before he could answer, all three were hit by a train.

What is the pope's phone number?

Et cum spiri 200.

*   *   *

At a Mafia funeral how can you tell the difference between members of the Mafia and the priest?

The priest is the one without the white tie.

*   *   *

Columbus Day: The Italian Yom Kippur.

*   *   *

Did you hear about the . . .

—Italian girl who had a wonderful way of protecting herself from Peeping Toms?

She kept her window shades up.

*   *   *

—Italian who bought a notebook to write down all his thoughts in?

Three years later he finished page one.

*   *   *

Did you hear about the ...

—Italian gynecologist who set up a dual practice?

He delivered pizzas and babies at the same time.

* * *

—Five-speed Italian tank used in World War II?

It had one speed forward and four in reverse.

* * *

—The Hollywood producer who wanted to give a new Italian actress a tremendous buildup—but nature beat him to it?

* * *

Did you hear about the ...

—Italian tanks?

They're the only one with backup lights.

* * *

—Italian Casanova who had a sofa spot in his heart for girls?

* * *

—Italian Chianti connoisseur?

He said, "Give me a glass of vino and I not only name a the year it was made but I tella you who jump ona the grapes."

* * *

—Italian girl who ran out of wool while knitting a sweater, so she finished it with spaghetti?

The first time she wore it two meat balls followed her home.

* * *

Did you hear about the ...

—Frenchman and the Italian who jumped off a building to commit suicide?

The Italian missed.

* * *

—Italian who spent an hour reading the label on a tomato can?

* * *

—Italian bookies who are finally getting even?

Last week they closed two police stations.

* * *

—Italian girl who was so ugly garlic backed away from her?

* * *

Did you hear about the . . .

—Italian who flunked his citizenship test because he couldn't spell D.D.T.

* * *

—Italian who committed suicide?

He jumped in front of a parked car.

* * *

—Italian who quit his job because he was selling baby carriages and the boss gave him virgin territory?

* * *

—Italian girl who stopped taking the pill because her husband went out and bought a condominium?

Did you hear about the ...

—Italian sports mechanic?

He fixes basketball games.

* * *

—Italian girl who has a terrible time in the morning?

She's so fat, she rocks herself to sleep trying to get up.

* * *

—Italian who died drinking milk?

The cow sat down on him.

* * *

—Italian immigrant who thought "Established 1891" was the company's phone number?

*   *   *

—Italian who was so conceited he put a mirror on his bathroom ceiling so he could watch himself gargle?

*   *   *

Did you hear about the ...

—Italian who couldn't make any money being a crook?

He robbed tourists on their way home from Las Vegas.

*   *   *

—Italian girl who was so thin, when she wore a fur coat she looked like a pipe cleaner?

*   *   *

—Italian who got a job as a mailman because he thought it was better than walking the streets?

*　　*　　*

—Italian hold-up man?

He sells brassieres.

*　　*　　*

Did you hear about the ...

—Italian who thought the St. Louis Cardinals were appointed by the pope?

*　　*　　*

—Two Scandori brothers?

One went into politics and the other went straight.

*　　*　　*

—Italian housewife who is so fat, when she takes a bath they have to grease the sides of the tub?

*　　*　　*

—Italian bricklayer who went crazy trying to lay a cornerstone in a roundhouse?

*   *   *

Did you hear about the...

—Italian boxer who has taken so many dives he's got a cauliflower stomach?

*   *   *

—Italian who makes his own sparkling burgundy? Uses two bottles of red wine and a bicycle pump.

*   *   *

—Italian woman who is so fat she uses inner tubes for garters?

*   *   *

—Italian who tried to keep his wife's cold from going from her head to her chest— so he tied a knot in her throat?

*   *   *

Did you hear about the ...

—Italian girl who was so fat she had to put her makeup on with a paint roller?

*   *   *

—Italian who broke his arm raking leaves?

He fell out of a tree.

*   *   *

—Italian bride who was murdered on her honeymoon?

On the first night she kneeled beside the bed and said, "Now I lay me down to sleep!"

*   *   *

—Italian starlet who wears black panties labeled: "Made In Hollywood—By Almost Everybody."

*   *   *

Did you hear about the . . .

—Italian girl who was called to the witness stand?

She whispered to her lawyer, "Must I bare everything?"
"No," he answered, "just cross your legs!"

* * *

—Italian showgirl who said she'd do anything for a mink coat and now she can't button it?

* * *

—Italian watching them catch tuna?

He said, "Isn't it a wonderful how they canna a squeeze those 200 pound fish into such a little a cans?"

* * *

Did you hear about the . . .

—Italian who was so skinny that when he took a shower he wore snowshoes?

* * *

—Italian girl who was so cockeyed she could watch a tennis match without moving her head?

* * *

—Maria the stenographer?

She walked into her boss's office and said, "I've got another position!" He said, "Fine, let's try it!"

* * *

—Italian who was told that in order to be a big success in America you had to make a killing in the stock market?

So he went out and killed a stockbroker.

* * *

Clarence Pine, Farmer's Market impressario, tells about the time Jascha Heifetz, the world famous violinist, was scheduled to play a concert at a small town in upstate New York. An elderly Italian farmer heard about it and drove fifty miles through a blinding snowstorm to be at the auditorium. Because of the inclement weather only fourteen people comprised the audience.

The violin virtuoso walked to center stage and apologized. "I'm terribly sorry," he said. "It is impossible for an artist to perform before such a small gathering. The management will be happy to refund your money. I hope that we shall meet again under much happier circumstances!"

"Wait a minute!" shouted the old farmer from the balcony. "I drove a fifty miles through a snow storma to hear a you! Please! Jascha! At leasta sing one song!"

*   *   *

Gabrelli and Benzini were watching a jet fly overhead. "Hey, atsa the pope up there!" declared Gabrelli.

"How you know dat?" asked Benzini.

"Atsa easy," replied the first Italian. The airaplane a say T W A. Topa Wop Aboard."

PASTA-FA-ALL

Why don't they give Italian elevator operators a ten-minute break?

Because they would have to retrain them.

* * *

Why did the Italian navy disband their underwater demolition team?

They kept leaving an oil slick.

* * *

At a recent Friars Roast, comedian Jackie Vernon told of his grandfather's arrival in the U.S.

"He came over on a cattle boat from Italy. He'd worked for years to get the passage money. He saved and saved and finally he arrived in New York.

As he was getting off the boat he saw a deep sea diver climbing out of the water onto the dock.

"How you lika dis?" said the old man. "I spend a money to take a da boat and this a guy he walk a over!"

*　　*　　*

Why does an Italian take his kid to the garbage dump?

To give him on-the-job training.

*　　*　　*

What do they call removing a splinter from an Italian's behind?

Brain surgery.

*　　*　　*

After the marriage ceremony of her only daughter, Mrs. Del Monte took the girl aside and gave her advice about the first night.

"Whata happens ina the bedroom is a very important," said the mother. "Tonight, you puta on a lotsa perfume. Sprinkle a powder ona the bed. Wear a reala

flimsy nightagown. You be ready when your man a comes to geta you!"

"Mama!" said the girl. "I know how to make love! How do you make lasagna!"

* * *

Why don't they allow Italians to swim in the Hudson River?

They leave a ring.

* * *

What is Italian matching luggage?

Two shopping bags from the A & P.

* * *

Tourist walked into a cannibal restaurant in Africa and said, "What's good on the menu today?"

"Well, we've got sauteed Frenchman for $3.95!" said the waiter.

"What else?" asked the customer.

"You can have roast breast of Englishman for $5.95."

"Anything else?"

"Yes, we have fried Italian at $16.50!"

"How come that's so much more expensive?" asked the tourist.

"You know how tough it is to clean one of them?" replied the waiter.

* * *

Chinese-Italian restaurant: Ming Chow Pizzeria.

* * *

The following humorous errors were supposedly made by school children in oral and written examinations on their knowledge of Italians.

Robinson Crusoe was a great operatic tenor.

* * *

The Merchant of Venice was a famous Italian who bought and sold canal boats.

* * *

A Latin Quarter is an Italian twenty-five cent piece.

* * *

History calls people Romans because they never stayed in one place.

*   *   *

Columbus sailed to America on *The Nina, The Pinta* and *The Santa Fe*.

*   *   *

Sign In Wine Factory:
Any Italian who wishes to attend the funeral of a relative must tell the foreman of his department on the day of the game.

*   *   *

Pasquale was being examined for naturalization as a U.S. citizen. "Who is the president of the United States?"

The foreigner answered correctly.

"And the vice president?"

Again he gave the right answer.

"Could you be president?"

"No! No!"

"Why not?"

"I'ma too busy. I worka in the barber shop alla day now."

*   *   *

73

How do you kill an Italian when he's drinking?

Close the toilet seat on him.

What is the smallest volume in the world?
Who's Who In Italy.

*   *   *

Diary of an Italian Girl on a Caribbean Cruise:

Monday: Was invited to dine at the captain's table.
Tuesday: Spent the day with the captain.
Wednesday: Captain made ungentlemanly proposals to me.
Thursday: Captain said he'd sink the ship if I didn't agree to his proposals.
Friday: Saved 500 lives.

*   *   *

Recording star, Tommy Leonetti, regales friends with this apocryphal tale about Giacomo Puccini, the celebrated opera composer:

Puccini once heard an organ grinder under his window playing excerpts from his work, *La Boheme*. The tempo was much too slow and the dragging notes drove the composer to distraction.

Finally, unable to bear it any longer, he

rushed into the street and told the musician, "Here, I am Puccini! I will show you how to play this music correctly."

He grabbed the crank handle of the organ, turned it rapidly for a few turns, and thus speeded up the tempo. "There," he said. "That is how it should be played."

The next day Puccini heard the organ grinder playing again. Looking out his window, Puccini saw that the organ grinder had a sign hanging over his hurdy-gurdy: "Pupil of Puccini."

*　　*　　*

Letter From Newly Arrived Immigrant:

Dear Mama:

They have a thing to wash in here call a bathatub. I have a trouble the firsta time I use it. A lot of water come out of the faucets and it kept a running down a hole in the bottom. Finally, I figure it out and everything was okay. I just a sit on the hole and washa at the same time.

Your loving son,
Luigi

*　　*　　*

Italian Buffalo: A Bison.

* * *

Salvatorelli arrived in America and in a short while his relatives taught him to say, "Apple pie and coffee" in English, so he could order in a restaurant. The next day the immigrant walked into a coffee shop. "What would you like?" asked the waitress. "Applea pie and a coffee," replied Salvatorelli.

Since that was all he could say, he was forced to eat apple pie and coffee every day for a week. When he complained to his cousins they taught him to say, "Ham sandwich."

Armed with the new addition to his vocabulary, Salvatorelli said to the waitress, "Ham sandwich."

"White or rye?" asked the girl.

"Applea pie and a coffee," said the Italian.

* * *

Why were the ancient Roman parents strict with their children?

The kids had to be back from every orgy by eleven o'clock.

* * *

At the Frontier Hotel in Las Vegas, comedian Dave Barry breaks up his audiences with these two beauts: "If you want to learn to speak Italian," says Dave, "all you need to know is one word: 'Atsa!' Atsa table! Atsa chair!..."

Mike Murphy and Dante Giordano were digging a ditch. "My brotha justa hada twins!" exclaimed the recent arrival from Calabria. "A boy and a girl!"

"Now that's nice to hear," replied the Son of Erin. "What did they call the girl?"

"Denise!" answered Dante.

"And what about the boy?" asked the Irishman.

"De nephew!" said the Italian proudly.

* * *

Scene in Rosselli's Restaurant:

Customer: Will my spaghetti be long?
Waiter: I dunno. We never measure it.

* * *

What did Donatelli do with his first fifty-cent piece?

He married her.

* * *

Why did the Italian lose his job as an elevator operator?

He couldn't learn the route.

Sign in a Rome Shop Window:

Don't be mistaken for an American tourist—wear Italian-made clothes.

* * *

For a wedding present, Rossano gave his son Mario $200. Two weeks later he asked him, "What you do witha the money?"

"I bought a wristwatch, papa!" answered the boy.

"Stupido!" cried his father. "You should'va bought a rifle!"

"A rifle? What for?"

"Suppose a some day you comea home anna find a man a sleepin'a wid you wife," explained Rossano. "What a you gonna do? Wake hima up and tella him what a time it is?"

* * *

Grandma Panzini had been voting in America for thirty years and finally decided to become a citizen. She arrived in court on the appointed day.

The first part of the test was on American history. The judge held up a picture of Abraham Lincoln and asked, "Who is this?"

"Dat's a Abraham Lincoln!" replied Mrs. Panzini.

His Honor then held up a picture of George Washington. "And who is this?" he inquired.

"Datsa his wife!" answered Grandma with pride.

*   *   *

This Could Only Happen In Italy Dept:

Kidnappers grabbed a little boy and two days later sent him home with the ransom note.

The parents sent the kid back with the money.

*   *   *

Where does an Italian hide his money?

Underneath the soap.

*   *   *

In the middle of shaving a customer, Bandini said, "Mista, you have a ketchup for a lunch?"

"No," answered the man.

"Then," said the barber, "I justa cuta you throat!"

*   *   *

The intestines of Dante Rossetti,
Were exceedingly frail and petty.
All he could eat,
Was finely chopped meat,
And all he could love is spaghetti.

*   *   *

Just after Mussolini took over as dictator he is reputed to have made this proclamation:

"Whata I wanta in disa country is a lessa whoopie and a more a wopie!"

*   *   *

Immigrant Candelli was digging ditches on one side of the street while 200 men worked on the other side. "How come you make a me work on this side alla time by myself?" asked the new arrival to America.

"You've got bad breath!" answered the foreman.

"Say, Mista!" retorted the Italian. "Ifa you kissed as many politicians as I did to a get thisa job, you'd have a bad breath a too!"

*   *   *

Sign On Garbage Truck:

"We Cater to Polish Weddings."

* * *

In order to get a job with the railroad, Angelo had to pass a test. "Suppose two trains were heading for each other at 100 miles per hour on the same track," asked the personnel manager, "What would you do?"

"I take a the red flag and wave a them to a stop," Angelo answered.

"But you don't have a red flag!" pointed out the man.

"Then I'ma take a the skwitcha iron and change a the tracks!"

"You don't have a switch iron either!"

"Well, in thata case," decided the Italian, "I'ma gonna call upa my wife, Maria!"

"What's your wife got to do with two trains coming at each other at 100 miles an hour," exclaimed the man in charge of hiring.

"I tella her to come down—cause she'sa gonna see the biggest a smash-up in the whole world!"

* * *

Polack: I not be dumb as I look!
Italian: You couldn't be!

For Sale

Italian underwater wet suits. Only been used once. On the inside.

*   *   *

Manetti and Guillemo came stumbling out of a saloon, carrying their buddy who had passed out.

"Throw him in the back of the truck!" said Manetti.

"Do you want him to fall out and get killed!" slobbered Guillemo. "Let him drive!"

*   *   *

A banker in a small town was bald. In the summer the flies attacked his pate, and in the winter the cold air made his hairless head uncomfortable. So he got into the habit of wearing a hat all day, even during the bank's business hours.

Now in this same small town lived an Italian workman who would come to the bank each week to get his paycheck cashed. "Why don't you open an account with us?" the banker asked one day.

The Italian looked at the banker's hat and then whispered, "I'm afraid, Mister Boss. You alla time looka like you gonna maybe take a tripa somewhere."

*　　*　　*

The most famous lovers of all time, as everybody knows, were Italian. Here's a little comic verse to help you remember:

> Twas in a restaurant they met,
> Romeo and Juliet.
> He had no cash to pay the debt,
> So Romeo'd what Juli'et.

*　　*　　*

Why do Italians talk with their hands?

Because they can't stand each other's breath.

*　　*　　*

Guiseppi wanted to write a letter to his wife. He said to his son, "Joe, tella me something, please?"

"What is it, Pop?"

"How you spell sence?"

"S-E-N-S-E."

"Naa, senca-a, sence. How you spella sence?"

"C-E-N-T-S," said his son.

"Naa, naa!"

"That's the only way I know. S-E-N-S-E or C-E-N-T-S."

"Naa. Looka, Joe. I'ma write your mamma in Asbury Park, and I wanna tell her nobody's a wash the dishes sence a last Thursday."

*   *   *

Why do Italian garbage men have it so good?

They get $50 a week and all they can eat.

*   *   *

The great composer, Rossini, went to see his doctor. After examining him, the physician said, "Your trouble stems from wine, women, and song."

"I can get along without the songs," declared Rossini, "since I compose my own."

"Well, which of the other two are you prepared to give up?" inquired the M.D.

"That depends entirely on the vintage," replied the celebrated composer.

*   *   *

Scene in Patsy's Pizzeria:

Customer: What time is it?
Waiter: I'ma sorry, this is a not a my
         station!

*   *   *

Sal and Frank were having a few brews
at the corner saloon. "My next door neighbor must think I'm in the Coast Guard,"
observed Sal.

"Why's that?" asked Frank.

"He keeps calling up my wife to ask if
the coast is clear!"

*   *   *

Columbus Day: A great holiday. Hundreds
            of years ago on this very
            day, Columbus discovered
            Ohio.

*   *   *

Antonio: Last night I had a nighta mare.
Angelo: Whata happened?
Antonio: I dreamta I was eating a spa-
         ghetti.
Angelo: Why's a that so bad?
Antonio: I woke up and a the string on a
         my pajamas was a gone.

*   *   *

Why does an Italian have a hole in his pants pocket?

So he can count to six.

How can you tell an Italian movie star from an American movie star?

She's the one with the moustache.

*   *   *

Alfredo and Guido sat down on the park bench to eat their lunch. Alfredo opened up his lunch box and said, "Sonama gun! Peanuts a butter sandwiches again! I hate a peanuts a butter!" And he threw them away.

After watching him do this for over a week, Guido said, "Hey, if you no like a peanuts a butter, how come you no tella your wife no make a you peanuts a butter?"

"Whata wife?" screamed Alfredo. "I makea my own sandwiches!"

*   *   *

Young man told his mother he wanted to get married. "Whats a dat?" she shouted. "Who's agon love you like mama? Who's agon wash you socks? Who's agon make you lasagna?"

"Ma, why're you talking like that?" asked the bewildered son. "We're not even Italian!"

*   *   *

Vince Scully, the Dodgers brilliant play-by-play broadcaster, broke up a Friars Club luncheon with this classic:

Octogenarian Romano was extolling the virtues of his new hearing aid. "I can hear a the bird from a 100 yards away," he said proudly. "I recognize a the tinkle of a bell from across a the street. I canna tell the blind man is a coming from the tapping of his a cane onna the sidewalk!"

"That's a wonderful!" offered his friend, Ferruccio. "What kind is it?"

"A quarter to three!" announced the old man.

* * *

Abe Harris, the premier pharmacist in Rocky River, Ohio, likes the story of the eighty-year-old Italian who went to a doctor and complained that he was becoming impotent.

"When did you first notice it?" asked the physician.

"Last night, and again this morning," replied the octogenarian.

* * *

An Italian was being examined for citizenship. The first question the judge asked was: "How many states are there in the union?"

"I dunno," replied the immigrant. "I ask you how many banan' in a bunch, you dunno. You know your biz, I know a mine."

*   *   *

A small plane was flying over Italy. As it flew over the Bay of Naples, the pilot said to his passenger, "Have you ever heard the expression: 'See Naples and die'?"

"Yes, I have, why?" answered the passenger.

"Well, take a good look," said the pilot. "The propeller just fell off."

*   *   *

Orchestra Leader Herb Silvers tells about the soldier in ancient Rome who was called off to war. Fearing for the safety of his beautiful young wife, he locked her in armor and gave the key to his best friend.

"If I do not return in six months," declared the warrior, "use the key. To you, and only you, do I entrust it!"

He galloped off to battle.

He'd only gone five miles when he heard hoof beats behind him. Through a cloud of dust appeared his closest friend, who shouted excitedly, "*Stop!* You gave me the wrong key!"

THE END . . .

of the Italian jokes, that is. Please turn the book over and start all over again, to read the Polish jokes. (Unless you're Italian, of course, in which case you should read this section again—only this time read the words between the pictures.)

NOTE

If you are Italian and find it
difficult to laugh at yourself or
if you have become angry,
there is one way to have a laugh and
lessen your anger. Follow these
instructions carefully: (1) Every
time you see the word *Italian*
(or any slang meaning same) substitute
one of the following words:
*Jewish, Irish, Chinese, German, British,
Icelandic, Brazilian, Canadian, Filipino, Hungarian,
Egyptian, Russian, Australian, Norwegian,
African, Korean, Gypsy, Afghanistanian,*
etc. See how easy it is to be funny!
(2) Now you can read the Polish jokes.
PS . . . Heard any good Jewish or Irish
jokes lately? We're doing another book,
and this time it's *their* turn.

3 CHEERS

FOR THE

ITALIANS!

(an unpaid political advertisement.)

JONATHAN SEGAL CHICKEN

"Chickens were not made to fly, Jonathan," the outraged flock told the plucky (yet unwilling to be plucked) rooster named Jonathan Segal Chicken. "You know what a chicken's fate is—to end up on a Melmac dinnerplate on Friday night, peering disconsolately from under the mashed potatoes and succotash."

But not for *Jonathan Segal Chicken*, the hero of the Sol Weinstein-Howard Albrecht paperback howler for Pinnacle Books. His mother laments, ("It's my fault. I never should have lined his nest with brochures from Eastern Airlines") and his father is irate, ("He's worse than your crazy brother Sidney Chicken, the one who fell in love with a weathervane . . . on a Baptist Church yet!").

Yes, it's *Jonathan Segal Chicken*, meeting four and twenty militant blackbirds in Harlem; learning how to divebomb statues better than any pigeon; avoiding the blandishments of Sir Lance-a-Lark, the Greenwich Village gay bird; fighting the evil Colonel Kentucky, the human who heads the murderous chicken pickin's restaurants, and finally facing his destiny by taking on five supersonic Communist MIGs in the warring skies over his beloved Israel.

For laughs, cackles, chuckles and smiles, plus all the philosophy even a certain seagull could never supply, it's *Jonathan Segal Chicken!*

If this book is not available where you bought this book, write to PINNACLE BOOKS, INC., enclosing $1.25 for each copy desired.

THE ODDFATHER

So you thought Mario Puzo had the real lowdown on the sinister world of the Mafia?

Forget it! The truth is in *The Oddfather*, that hood-happy satire by Sol Weinstein and Howard Albrecht, who outdo Mario Puzo by really making an offer you can't refuse!

Follow Don Provolone, the big cheese in the Mafia and his crazy sons, Fungi the Rapist, Carmine the Cretin and Nicholas the Sensitive, into this narrative of betrayal, murder, sex and spaghetti. Meet his enemies, Don Knottso, the Nervous Don; Don Cherrie, the Golfing Don; Don Rickeleoni, the Insulting Don! Watch Don Provolone take a "contract" from the President of the United States for the next war in Southeast Asia! Thrill to Fungi's love life as he makes more penetrations than the Dallas Cowboy's linebackers! The laughs fly as fast as the bullets from the Don's gun in The Oddfather, and you'll either be rolling on the ground or buried in it. (Choose one.)

Master comedy writers Sol Weinstein and Howard Albrecht, who gave you *Oh, Henry* and *Jonathan Segal Chicken,* now lay bare the mob in *The Oddfather!* Another howler from Pinnacle Books!